Evidence-Based Science Activities in Grades 3–5

This new book shows elementary teachers how evidence-based science activities help students achieve deeper conceptual understanding. Drawing on a wealth of research, authors Patrick Brown and James Concannon demonstrate how direct, hands-on experience in the science classroom can enable your students to become more self-reliant learners. They also provide a plethora of model lessons aligned with the Next Generation Science Standards (NGSS) and offer advice on how to create your lesson plans and activities to satisfy the demands of your curriculum. With the resources in this book, you and your students will be able to ditch the textbook and embark upon an exciting and rewarding journey to scientific discovery.

Dr. Patrick L. Brown, Ph.D., is the Executive Director of STEM and Career Education for the Fort Zumwalt School District in O'Fallon, Missouri.

Dr. James P. Concannon, Ph.D., is the Director of the School of Education at William Woods University in Fulton, Missouri.

Also Available by Routledge Eye On Education
www.routledge.com/eyeoneducation

Inquiry-Based Science Activities in Grades 6–12:
Meeting the NGSS
Patrick Brown and James Concannon

STEM by Design: Strategies and Activities for Grades 4–8
Anne Jolly

The STEM Coaching Handbook: Working with Teachers to Improve Instruction
Terry Talley

Creating Scientists: Teaching and Assessing Science Practice for the NGSS
Christopher Moore

Writing Science Right: Strategies for Teaching Scientific and Technical Writing
Sue Neuen and Elizabeth Tebeaux

Write, Think, Learn: Tapping the Power of Daily Student Writing Across the Content Areas
Mary K. Tedrow

Evidence-Based Science Activities in Grades 3–5

Meeting the NGSS

Dr. Patrick L. Brown and Dr. James P. Concannon

Routledge
Taylor & Francis Group
NEW YORK AND LONDON

First published 2019
by Routledge
52 Vanderbilt Avenue, New York, NY 10017

and by Routledge
2 Park Square, Milton Park, Abingdon, Oxon, OX14 4RN

Routledge is an imprint of the Taylor & Francis Group, an informa business

© 2019 Taylor & Francis

The right of Patrick Brown and James Concannon to be identified as authors of this work has been asserted by them in accordance with sections 77 and 78 of the Copyright, Designs and Patents Act 1988.

All rights reserved. No part of this book may be reprinted or reproduced or utilised in any form or by any electronic, mechanical, or other means, now known or hereafter invented, including photocopying and recording, or in any information storage or retrieval system, without permission in writing from the publishers.

Trademark notice: Product or corporate names may be trademarks or registered trademarks, and are used only for identification and explanation without intent to infringe.

Library of Congress Cataloging-in-Publication Data
Names: Brown, Patrick, 1978– author. | Concannon, James, author.
Title: Evidence-based science activities in grades 3–5 : meeting the NGSS / Patrick L. Brown and James Concannon.
Description: New York : Routledge, 2019. | Includes bibliographical references.
Identifiers: LCCN 2018039348 (print) | LCCN 2018051763 (ebook) | ISBN 9780815383444 (ebook) | ISBN 9780815383390 | ISBN 9780815383390 (hardback) | ISBN 9780815383420 (paperback) | ISBN 9780815383444 (ebook)
Subjects: LCSH: Science—Study and teaching (Elementary)—United States. | Inquiry-based learning—United States. | Next Generation Science Standards (Education)
Classification: LCC Q183.3.A1 (ebook) | LCC Q183.3.A1 B767 2019 (print) | DDC 372.35/044—dc23
LC record available at https://lccn.loc.gov/2018039348

ISBN: 978-0-8153-8339-0 (hbk)
ISBN: 978-0-8153-8342-0 (pbk)
ISBN: 978-0-8153-8344-4 (ebk)

Typeset in Palatino
by Apex CoVantage, LLC

Dedication

To my best friends, Greg and Tim—PB

To my graduate advisor, Dr. Lloyd Barrow—JC

Many of the lesson plans in this book were originally published in *Science Activities: Classroom Projects and Curriculum Ideas*, a peer-reviewed journal that provides teachers and educators with the best classroom-tested projects, experiments, and curriculum ideas that promote scientific inquiry through active learning experiences.

For more information about *Science Activities*, including tips on how to prepare and submit a manuscript for publication, visit: http://tandfonline.com/action/journalInformation?show=aimsScope&journalCode=vsca20.

Contents

Meet the Authors ix
Foreword by Dr. Norman G. Lederman xi
Preface by Patrick Brown and James Concannon xiii
Acknowledgments xv
Introduction by Patrick Brown and James Concannon xvii

1. What Are the Features of Evidence-Driven Science Activities? 1
   Patrick Brown and James Concannon

2. Sequencing Science Instruction as a Pathway to Evidence-Driven Science Activities 7
   Patrick Brown and James Concannon

3. Using Classroom Inquiry as a Pathway to Evidence-Driven Science Activities 13
   Patrick Brown and James Concannon

4. Using Phenomenon-Based Teaching as a Pathway to Evidence-Driven Science Activities 19
   Patrick Brown and James Concannon

5. Connecting to Contemporary National Science Standards 25
   Patrick Brown and James Concannon

6. Engage Students in Designing Experiments so Hands-on Science Does Not Spiral Out of Control 33
   Patrick Brown

7. Students Use of the PSOE Model to Understand Weather and Climate 41
   Patrick Brown and James Concannon

8. Two-Liter Bottles and Botanical Gardens: Using Inquiry to Learn Ecology 49
   Patrick Brown, Patricia Friedrichsen, and Lou Mongler

9. Enhancing Elementary Students' Experiences Learning About Circuits Using an Exploration-Explanation Instructional Sequence 55
   Patrick Brown and Tim Brown

10. Elementary Students' Investigations in Natural Selection 61
    Nancy Bartley, James Concannon, and Patrick Brown

11. Lessons Learned.. 75
    Patrick Brown and James Concannon

Meet the Authors

Dr. Patrick L. Brown, Ph.D., is the Executive Director of STEM and Career Education for the Fort Zumwalt School District in O'Fallon, Missouri. He has a range of educational experiences and has taught middle and high school science classes as well as undergraduate and graduate courses for teachers. Dr. Brown has received awards for his methods course teaching such as the Lambda Chi Alpha Professor of the Year and the Excellence in Teaching Award from the College of Education at the University of Missouri–Columbia. His area of research deals with strategies for enhancing science literacy and teacher professional development. He has several publications that appear as journal articles, book chapters, and books and he has given many presentations at the regional, national, and international level.

Dr. James P. Concannon, Ph.D., is the Director of Education at William Woods University in Fulton, Missouri. Since earning his Ph.D. in science education from the University of Missouri–Columbia in 2008, Dr. Concannon has taught elementary, middle, and secondary science methods to K–12 prospective teachers. Dr. Concannon has collaborated extensively with Dr. Patrick Brown since their days in graduate school at the University of Missouri. Before graduate school, Dr. Concannon taught high school zoology, physics, environmental science, and chemistry.

Foreword

In the past three decades there have been no fewer than three major reform documents in science education: *Benchmarks for Science Literacy* (1993), *National Science Education Standards* (1996), and *Next Generation Science Standards* (2013). Each of these reform documents has justifiably (based on current research on science teaching and learning) advocated that science teaching should use an inquiry approach in which students are allowed to ask questions, develop research designs to answer their questions, collect data, and use their data to arrive at conclusions and answers to their questions. Using the terminology in the field, teachers are expected to place students in situations in which they are free to construct science knowledge. This is what constructivist epistemology advocates as the most effective way to teach science. In short, students are expected to learn science in the same way that scientists develop understandings of the natural world. These recommendations are in stark contrast to what is typically observed in science classrooms at the K–12 levels.

In general, regardless to the varied science education reforms, science teachers tend to rely heavily on the textbooks they use because this is the way they were taught science. Further, at the elementary level, the target audience of this book, teachers are insecure about the subject matter they know. The reform documents have been relatively ineffective in transforming science teaching because teachers have not been provided with effective professional development or with resources that are research based, concrete, and easily accessible. This book by Patrick Brown and Jim Concannon is a significant contribution to helping teachers achieve the vision of current science education reforms. It provides teachers with what they need.

There is no shortage of teacher resources that claim to be inquiry oriented and aligned with current reform documents. More often than not, these resources are the musings of science education professionals with little or no classroom teaching experience. Both authors are experienced teachers, and the activities provided in the book are all research based and classroom tested. The book will assist teachers in not only providing reform-based science instruction, but also science instruction that easily integrates attention to English language support. In addition to providing a sound grounding in the learning theory that supports current visions of science teaching, the instructional activities are good examples of hands-on and minds-on experiences for students. All too often, it is assumed that if students are experiencing hands-on activities, they are involved in inquiry. Research has shown that this is not the case, but the sample activities provided in the following pages also insure that students are mentally engaged as well as physically engaged.

Although the familiar learning cycle is a foundation of the authors' perception of effective instruction, they also provide a unique acknowledgment that there is no single way to have students engaged in evidence-based activities. Three different pathways are offered to accomplish this end. For example, teachers may choose to engage their students in a phenomenon-based experience or a formal problem-based activity. This provides teachers with the flexibility they need to facilitate the science learning of their students. Although it should be an intuitive idea, it is not typically communicated to teachers that there is no singularly best way to teach science effectively.

The book provides a good balance between theoretical foundations of effective teaching and learning and practical, classroom-tested instructional activities. Obviously, the book cannot, and should not, provide teachers with a full curriculum for the school year. But, it does show what is possible and provides teachers with a productive starting point. As the authors state, there is no need for teachers to remain tied to the textbook that they have ordered or the textbook that someone else has ordered. Certainly, a textbook provides structure for students and the teacher. Good instruction is so much more, however. In this sense, the authors have delivered what they have promised.

Dr. Norman G. Lederman

Preface

Patrick Brown and James Concannon

We all have unique activities and demonstrations and improve upon them every year. We may not remember where we found the original idea—perhaps it was from a colleague, a mentor, a textbook, or a professional journal—but they have become a favorite among students. The model lessons presented here within have been a favorite among our students and lead to long-lasting conceptual understanding. We firmly believe they became favorites because the learning experience emphasized constructing knowledge and students self-directing their development of skills and knowledge. Older students come back and tell us they remember the activities we attribute to them having an intellectual stake in learning and have created complex cognitive structures created by the combination of hands-on, minds-on experiences.

In this book, we tried to capture the most potent pedagogical practices that we use to teach elementary students and that we use in our elementary methods courses. We have supported these practices with model lessons. Our approach is not so much to create a new activity that never existed from scratch but to firmly ground activities in the science education and cognitive science research and test it with young kids.

This book is meant to be a companion to our middle-level publication titled *Inquiry-Based Science Activities in Grades 6–12*. Many of the activities originated in our practices as middle-level and high school teachers, and we adapted these lessons for elementary students and teachers. We found we could accomplish quite a lot by shifting the content focus and teaching appropriate science practices by using activities we had previously used with older students. In this regard, what serves as an introductory lesson for elementary students can be a springboard to more advanced studies in middle school and beyond. A similar activity, with a different focus, can have a substantial impact on students' abilities to transfer ideas and apply knowledge in different contexts. Remember, we had a good reason for adapting our middle and high school activities to elementary—we had learned they were student favorites and the lessons helped developed long-term science understanding.

Although there are similar activities with different content focuses, there is quite a bit this book offers that is not in the middle-level version. We have gone into considerably more detail and provide planning strategies for what we advocate as three pathways to evidence-driven activities. Also, we dedicate some time to showing how science learning can naturally be combined with English Language Arts to help students transfer writing skills in authentic situations.

Every teacher has his or her particular reasons for using specific classroom activities. Our motivation has always been to tap into students' love for learning science and then to design instruction so it helps students learn science best, by using the research in science education that we call pathways. We hope that the ideas presented lend new insight into ways to make elementary science even more impactful for students.

Acknowledgments

We thank Lauren Davis, Senior Editor at Routledge, and her team for their excellent editorial work. We also thank the Editors and Reviewers of *Science Activities: Classroom Projects and Curriculum Ideas*.

Introduction

Patrick Brown and James Concannon

Promoting evidence-based inquiry in the classroom is a lot like building a bridge. Whether the bridge is an arch, beam, suspension, or cable-stayed, the signature feature—ability to support objects from point A to B—is of utmost importance. Bridge builders are accountable for ensuring bridges do not "fail under loading." They need to consider the strength, weight, and cost of materials, resonance due to stress, and fluctuations because of temperature and wind changes. We want our science classes to be like bridge building—supportive and providing connective learning experiences for students learning science. Evidence-driven science activities are built on the premise that teachers must scaffold classroom activities so students use their immediate experiences with data and evidence (Point A) to arrive at a scientifically accurate claim about the phenomenon under study (Point B).

We cannot highlight enough the analogy that evidence-driven science activities are like a bridge. A remarkable thing occurs for students when teachers use evidence-driven science activities. Students' direct experiences and the claims they construct serve as the basis for their scientific understanding. Also, students' evidence-based claims act as an easy entry point for introducing key science vocabulary, concepts, and supporting ideas at a meaningful time. From a cognitive standpoint, students' conceptual understanding of science is linked directly to their experiences with data and evidence. Teachers open opportunities for students to experience essential science practices when they sequence lessons where students have opportunities to collect data and use as evidence to support conclusions. Additional student-centered elaborations after making evidence-based claims should be directly connected to students' experiences. This elaboration process is critical because it allows students to develop much more productive and sophisticated ways of thinking about the world based on their direct experiences requiring students to transfer knowledge to new and unique situations. Thus, evidence-driven science activities empower students with deep conceptual understanding and cultivate the skills kids need to be more self-reliant learners.

How to Use This Book

This book grew out of our work as classroom science teachers with K–12 students. Through purposeful and intentional lesson planning, we learned important aspects of instructional design that have broad implications for learning.

In Chapter 1, we provide a short but informative description of essential ideas concerning learners and learning. Also, we believe a significant goal of evidence-driven science activities should be to get students to a place where they can make evidence-based claims. We describe the Claims-Evidence-Reasoning (C-E-R) framework that we use with students that cuts across the three different research-based pathways used to promote evidence-based activities. Elementary teachers will appreciate the attention of the C-E-R framework because it is an interdisciplinary bridge to English Language Arts (ELA) and the Common Core Standards (CCSS) (National Governors Association Center for Best Practices [NGA] and Council of Chief State School Officers [CCSSO] 2010).

Chapter 2, "Sequencing Science Instruction as a Pathway to Evidence-Driven Science Activities," discusses the vital role that hands-on, minds-on experiences with data and teacher explanations play in science learning. We share an optimal sequence for pairing hands-on experiences with explanations, as well as some tips for lesson planning.

In Chapter 3, "Using Classroom Inquiry as a Pathway to Evidence-Driven Science Activities," we discuss how the essential features of classroom inquiry and their variations allow for a whole host of implementation possibilities. We also provide a strategy we have used with many students and teachers so classrooms can design their unique inquiry investigations.

Then, in Chapter 4, "Using Phenomenon-Based Teaching as a Pathway to Evidence-Driven Science Activities," we show to create a meaningful and relevant context for learning. We have a few planning tips for picking phenomena to guide learning as well as critical components of a phenomenon-based lesson. Chapters 2–4 work well when combined.

Next, Chapter 5, "Connecting to Next Generation Science Standards," shows how the three research-based pathways naturally translate into the NGSS. We discuss the architecture of the NGSS and offer suggestions for teachers on how to use this book to begin the delve deeper into understanding the NGSS.

In Chapters 6–10, we provide model lessons that illustrate one or more of the pathways to evidence-driven science activities. We have used all of the lessons with students to address elementary standards. Teachers can go back and forth between the research chapters and the NGSS chapters when reading the model to develop their abilities to understand science teaching and learning from a more pedagogical viewpoint.

Finally, Chapter 11, "Lessons Learned," provides some key aspects to consider when creating evidence-driven science activities in your unique teaching contexts. The last chapter summarizes many of the key ideas presented in the book.

The ideas presented in the chapters were tested with elementary students and through teacher professional development and our work with prospective teachers in science methods courses. In the following, we share many of our lessons learned along the way.

Examples: Teacher Professional Development

Many teachers use demonstrations to teach science content only to discover that they do not have the lasting impact on students' understanding of the content. We have found success by supporting teachers to restructure demonstrations in instructional sequences that promote students making evidence-based claims. In one lesson presented here, students use the PSOE model to understand weather and climate. We used a PSOE sequence of instruction that included the following phases: Predict, Share, Observe, and Explain. In the PSOE phases, students first commit to an outcome based on their prior knowledge. Then students explore before they explain the outcome. This instructional sequence taps into students' prior knowledge. Also, by having students observe before explaining, the PSOE sequence is a natural pathway helping to drive students' evidence-based claims. During the weather and climate demonstration, students developed a long-lasting understanding of the transfer of energy and "convection" currents. Many teachers we have worked with notice that simple shifts in the arrangement of activities, such as doing a demonstration before explaining new content, is a way to promote deep conceptual understanding. Teachers like the PSOE model because students construct knowledge firsthand based on their experiences with data. The tried-and-true model lesson easily translates to the three dimensions of the Frameworks and Next Generation Science Standards (NGSS) and is based on research on how to sequence science instruction to optimize learning (Bybee 2002).

Examples: Beginning Teachers

One of the most significant challenges beginning teachers face is seamlessly transitioning from one lesson to the next. The model lesson "Engage Students in Designing Experiments so Hands-on Does Not Spiral Out of Control" is one example of how to structure multiple days' worth of instruction to support learning. In this model lesson, an inquiry-based approach teaches fundamental concepts associated with force and motion. Beginning teachers should take note that throughout this model lesson, one of the most powerful learning experiences occurs whereby students create their classroom investigation and then collect data to generate scientifically accurate claims. Once students have constructed knowledge and articulated it in their own words, the teacher can connect new terms, key ideas, and other related concepts to students' foundational knowledge. In this regard, beginning teachers benefit from the structure of the model lesson because it is an explicit example of how to construct lessons in accordance to how students learn science best (Bransford, Brown, and Cocking 2000).

Conclusions

We have used all of the model lessons with elementary students (and many teachers). The model lessons can easily be implemented in classroom settings, through professional development experiences, or in science methods courses. Teachers at all stages of the professional continuum benefit from reflecting on the activities and effectiveness of the lessons individually and in groups. Teachers have commented that the model lessons are a starting point for reflecting on learning and provide them with a plethora of ideas for their classroom. For many, implementing and reflecting on the model lessons has helped develop their professional knowledge of learners and learning, instructional activities, and understanding of content. In addition, numerous teachers successfully adapt these ideas to design their own unique evidence-driven inquires for students.

Further Reading

Bransford, J., A. Brown, and R. Cocking. 2000. *How people learn: Brain, mind, experience, and school*. Washington, DC: The National Academies Press.

Bybee, R., ed. 2002. *Learning science and the science of learning*. Arlington, VA: National Science Teachers Association Press.

National Governors Association Center for Best Practices & Council of Chief State School Officers (NGA/CCSSO). 2010. *The Common Core State Standards for English Language Arts & Literacy in History/Social Studies, Science, and Technical Subjects. Appendix A: Research Supporting Key Element of the Standards*. Washington, DC: Author.

1

What Are the Features of Evidence-Driven Science Activities?

Patrick Brown and James Concannon

Learning about learning can be both eye-opening and exciting. In particular, understanding how students construct knowledge and their innate reasoning abilities is vital to effective science teaching. These intricate and complex subjects can be one of the most exciting challenges of teaching. Many individuals have made substantial contributions to our understanding of how students learn science best, and the knowledge base is still growing as we better learn about factors that influence cognition. The well-established consensus is that students learn science best when they have opportunities to construct knowledge (termed *constructivism*) related to their prior experiences and ideas.

Learning theory and the innate skills that students bring to school and science classrooms can go hand in hand. Kids love to explore the world and explain how nature works. They form ideas about the causes for the changing of the seasons, create theories about the phases of the moon, and try to describe why they have some physical characteristics like their parents. These are just a few of the many science areas that students have ideas about based on their experiences. Students at a very early age think logically about their environment and look for patterns and relationships to construct explanations for science. Regardless of the accuracy of their ideas, students' immediate experiences are the basis for how they know and understand the world. From a very early age, students construct knowledge of scientific phenomena.

While students' scientific understandings can be a great starting point for instruction, they can also act as a barrier to gaining knowledge. Research in the cognitive sciences and science education demonstrates the implications of students' prior knowledge, and particularly their misconceptions, on learning (Bransford, Brown, and Cocking 2000). Prior knowledge is an important consideration in teaching, and students' incoming ideas, including misconceptions, must be addressed for them to gain a more accurate and complete scientific understanding. In fact, many resources identify typical misconceptions in many different science disciplines (see Driver, Squires, Rushworth, and Wood-Robinson 1994), and several books offer engaging ways to elicit students' science views (see Keeley and Tugel 2009; Keeley, Eberle, Tugel, and Dorsey 2008; Keeley, Eberle, and Tugel 2007; Keeley, Eberle, and Farrin 2005).

The reason prior knowledge is so necessary for teaching relates back to the early 1980s and conceptual change research. This continued line of research clearly shows that the most potent and influential instructional sequences require a purposeful interaction between students' incorrect or partially incomplete ideas with direct experiences to develop more plausible, intelligible, and fruitful explanations (Posner, Strike, Hewson, and Gertzog 1982). For students to accommodate new information, they must first become dissatisfied with their current conceptions. Many times teachers can promote dissatisfaction by providing opportunities for students to collect data and scientific evidence that cannot be explained when students rely upon their incomplete understandings. Learning facts is not enough to improve students' understanding of science. To understand science, students need opportunities to view new ideas in broader contexts of meaning. More recently, several scholarly books provide research supporting constructivist approaches and advocate building on students' prior knowledge in authentic learning situations (see Duschl, Schweingruber, and Shouse 2007; Michaels, Shouse, and Schweingruber 2008).

From a conceptual change perspective, instruction should start with assessing students' incoming ideas. If a teacher's entry point into a lesson does not begin with students' prior knowledge, conceptual misunderstandings may arise whereby students assimilate new information to their existing inaccurate foundation of knowledge (Posner, Strike, Hewson, and Gertzog 1982). By knowing students' prior knowledge and experiences, teachers can choose the best types of experiences to create dissatisfaction. The best experiences are ones whereby students are provided evidence-based experiences to construct knowledge. The logic is simple. If students have reliable and valid experiences that produce data and evidence, and students construct knowledge based on the evidence, then their conceptual understanding is based on their firsthand experiences. From a neurological standpoint, students' knowledge is firmly entrenched in their brains because they developed the ideas firsthand. Students have an enormous capacity to reason at very sophisticated levels from teaching approaches that productively scaffold their developing content knowledge and science reasoning skills.

Evidence-Driven Science Activities

If the ultimate goal is for students to derive understanding from experiences, then we must carefully consider our professional practices. While hands-on learning can naturally be engaging for students, the experiences must be carefully woven into the flow of instruction to produce the desired outcomes. What are the desired incomes? A significant finding from America's Lab report is that many students view science as a "false dichotomy," meaning that students think that the hands-on, "doing" part of science is separate from content (Singer, Hilton, and Schweingruber 2006). As a result, the desired outcomes are for students to discard incorrect ideas, accept the most accurate scientific explanations, and for students to learn the nature by which these science explanations are generated. Evidence-driven science activities allow teachers to meet these goals by first providing students with immediate experiences to form accurate understandings; and second, by connecting student's claims to scientifically accepted explanations. Connections happen when teachers purposefully link evidence from explorations to evidence-based explanations. Lectures, readings, and discussions can further support explanations. In sum, evidence-driven science activities require a unique combination of students' evidence-based experiences, students' scientific claims, and the teacher connecting students' claims to our current understandings of scientific phenomena.

Because student construction of knowledge is imperative to learning, we need to get students to the point from our classroom experience that they can accurately explain some vital aspect of the desired content from data and evidence gleaned from firsthand experiences. In other words, we need to push students to intellectually engage with data and evidence from hands-on experiences in a way that promotes long-lasting understanding. One highly beneficial way to promote student science learning, and learning in general, is to use writing in science. Instructional approaches that integrate science and other areas are supported by cognitive science research that suggests students need to organize ideas in meaningful and relevant ways (Donovan and Bransford 2005).

Claims-Evidence-Reasoning (C-E-R)

The sequence of students having inquiry experiences that produce data and evidence, forming claims about what happened, supporting claims with data, and justifying why the data supports the claim is the goal of evidence-driven science activities. There are multiple benefits to having students write in science, and research shows that students who engage in explaining ideas learn science better than students who only record ideas (Hand, Prain, and Yore 2001).

Regarding the three components (claims, evidence, and reasoning), students' claims typically represent what they can explain on a conceptual level about science. Students' claims are not factoids and typically are big ideas relevant to the discipline. Students claims are dependent on their experiences with evidence.

Evidence represents the accumulation of convincing data that supports the claim and is more than just one data point. One of the critical aspects in having students use evidence to make claims is to think logically about patterns, trends, and any relationships present in data. Once students have reliable data, they need to make sense of the information. Students benefit from thinking about the high and low data points across multiple trials and whether different factors change or remain the same in the investigation.

The reasoning statement asks students to explain the underlying scientific principles associated with the phenomena under study. Constructing reasoning statements is challenging because it requires students to link the evidence with the overarching claim and then explain the broader underlying scientific principles. Creating the reasoning statement might require discussions of appropriate scientific principles to explain the claim-evidence link. Some students struggle with explaining scientific principles, and helping them co-construct these ideas during teacher explanations is a way to build their understanding. From a cognitive standpoint, constructing the reasoning with students in light of their evidence-based claims is a way to entrench ideas and helps them develop sound reasoning skills and conceptual understanding. Thus, constructing the reasoning statement with students is a way to integrate labs and other forms of instruction like labs and lectures and textbook readings (McNeill and Krajcik 2012).

If students have done the hard intellectual work of constructing an evidence-based claim, then teachers can promote a more profound understanding by building a reasoning statement with their classes. What teachers should keep in mind is that many times the scientific principles that constitute the rationale can go beyond the investigation students are presently conducting. Many times, the scientific principles may have taken scientists hundreds of years to invent and involved numerous different investigations. Constructing the rationale with students allows them to place what they have learned in a broader framework for understanding to have a more coherent understanding.

Through our work with many students and teachers, we arrive at claims-evidence-reasoning through research-based instructional practices referred to here as pathways. Each of the model lessons (Chapters 6–10) illustrate how students can create evidence-based claims and how teachers can introduce scientific terminology that defines the principles and concepts. For example, in Chapter 7, "Students Use of the PSOE to Understand Weather and Climate," you will learn how to sequence a demonstration so students understand thermal energy flow. The principle and science term that describes energy flow is *convection* and introduced by the teacher after students have constructed conceptual knowledge based on firsthand evidence. Introducing the term *convection* in light of students' firsthand experiences is an intense time in learning and helps develop their scientific vocabulary in context. The model lessons show how using a research-based pathway allows students to construct C-E-R statements.

As teachers become more familiar with each of our approaches, aspects of each pathway become evident in the model lessons that allow students to construct evidence-based claims. Reflecting on the model lessons in respects to the three pathways helps develop knowledge of one approach and will strengthen teachers' abilities to design lessons using multiple pathways in tandem. The end goal is to use one pathway on its own or in combination with another, tied to every lesson taught.

Further Reading

Bransford, J., A. Brown, and R. Cocking. 2000. *How people learn: Brain, mind, experience, and school*. Washington, DC: The National Academies Press.

Donovan, M.S., and J.D. Bransford. 2005. *How students learn: History, mathematics, and science on the classroom*. Washington, DC: The National Academies Press.

Driver, R., A. Squires, P. Rushworth, and V. Wood-Robinson. 1994. *Making sense of secondary science*. London: Routledge.

Duschl, R.A., H.A. Schweingruber, and A.W. Shouse, eds. 2007. *Taking science to school: Learning and teaching science in grades K—8*. Washington, DC: The National Academies Press.

Hand, B., V. Prain, and L. Yore. 2001. Sequential writing tasks' influence on science writing. In *Writing as a learning tool: Integrating theory and practice*, eds. P. Tynjala, L. Mason, and K Lonka. Dordrecht, The Netherlands: Kluwer.

Keeley, P., and J. Tugel. 2009. *Uncovering student ideas in science. 25 New formative assessment probes*. Vol. 4. Arlington, VA: National Science Teachers Association Press.

Keeley, P., F. Eberle, and L. Farrin. 2005. *Understanding student ideas in science. 25 Formative assessment probes*. Vol. 1. Arlington, VA: National Science Teachers Association Press.

Keeley, P., F. Eberle, and J. Tugel. 2007. *Understanding student ideas in science. 25 more formative assessment probes*. Vol. 2. Arlington, VA: National Science Teachers Association Press.

Keeley, P., F. Eberle, J. Tugel, and C. Dorsey. 2008. *Uncovering student ideas in science. Another 25 formative assessment probes*. Vol. 3. Arlington, VA: National Science Teachers Association Press.

McNeill, K.L., and J. Krajcik. 2012. *Supporting grade 5–8 students in constructing explanations in science: The claim, evidence and reasoning framework for talk and writing*. New York: Pearson Allyn & Bacon.

Michaels, S., A.W. Shouse, and H.A. Schweingruber. 2008. *Ready, set, science! Putting research to work in K-8 science classrooms*. Board on Science Education, Center for Education, Division of Behavioral and Social Science and Education. Washington, DC: The National Academies Press. www.nap.edu/catalog/11882/ready-set-science-putting-research-to-work-in-k-8#toc

Posner, G.J., K.A. Strike, P.W. Hewson, and W.A. Gertzog. 1982. Accommodation of a scientific conception: Toward a theory of conceptual change. *Science Education*, 66, 211–227.

Singer, S.R., M.L. Hilton, and H.A. Schweingruber, eds. 2006. *America's lab report: Investigations in high school science*. Washington, DC: The National Academies Press.

2

Sequencing Science Instruction as a Pathway to Evidence-Driven Science Activities

Patrick Brown and James Concannon

Science instruction should be sequenced where students explore before teachers introduce science terminology, ideas, or concepts. We call this explore-before-explain teaching and can be accomplished through tried-and-true sequences of instruction such as the learning cycle. The learning cycle includes three sequential phases: (1) exploration, (2) invention (term introduction), (3) discovery (concept application) (Karplus and Their 1967). When employing the learning cycle, students have experiences with data (exploration) that is then used by students to construct accurate evidence-based claims (the student portion of the invention phase). Students' evidence-based claims are the foundation for their understanding and used to introduce key science terms, concepts, and supporting ideas (the teacher portion of the invention phase). Once students have constructed knowledge and have official explanations (e.g., teacher lectures, textbook readings, and discussions that occur during the teacher portion of the invention phase), they are given the opportunity to practice and test out new knowledge in new and different situations (i.e. "discovery phase") (Atkin and Karplus, 1962). Thus, the learning cycle places primacy on students' exploratory experiences, from which they construct some aspect of scientific knowledge on a conceptual level. Student constructed knowledge serves as an "anchor" for learning related topics.

Studies have compared the learning cycle to variations that sequence the teachers' explanation and the beginning of instruction and use investigations to verify provided ideas. As a result of a learning cycle process, students use science vocabulary accurately and can explain valid and reliable ways to generate ideas about their everyday world. This line of scholarship shows the learning cycle sequence is more effective at promoting science achievement, motivation, and encouraging scientific reasoning versus any other variation (Abraham and Renner 1986; Purser and Renner 1983; Renner, Abraham, and Birnie 1988). Abraham and Renner (1986) investigated student learning when experiencing different instructional sequences that all included the three learning cycle phases. They found when the invention phase was placed second, it was superior to other sequences in content achievement. Also, research on the necessity of each phase demonstrated that all three phases are essential for learning science concepts (Abraham 1992). Because of the alignment of the learning cycle with constructivist learning theories, an elementary curriculum has been designed (e.g., Science Curriculum Improvement Study [SCIS]) and demonstrated to be a useful approach (Shymansky, Kyle, and Alport 1983).

Since the initial invention of the learning cycle, other models have retained the exploration before explanation sequences such as the POE (Predict, Observe, and Explain) and 5Es (Engagement, Exploration, Explanation, Elaboration, and Evaluation) (Bybee 1997). The POE is a one-to-two-day explore-before-explain instructional model, whereas the 5E is a multiday instructional sequence. We share an example of a POE model that is one day in Chapter 7, and examples of multiday 5E lessons in Chapters 8, 9, and 10. The 5E builds on the learning cycle to add an engagement phase that precedes the learning cycle and an evaluation phase at the end of the learning cycle. The additional phases the 5E provides are based on advances in cognitive science that highlight the pivotal role that prior knowledge and reflecting on developing understanding plays in learning (Bransford, Brown, and Cocking, 2000; Bybee et al. 2006). By sequencing lessons using explore-before-explain instructional models, teachers can create a student-centered learning environment where students ask questions, plan and conduct investigations, gather data, and make evidence-based explanations.

Planning Tips for Learning Cycle Teaching

A critical learning cycle planning activity is to home in on the types of first-hand activities and data student can collect that allow them to construct accurate knowledge. Thus, teachers must plan a hands-on activity (lab, demonstration, investigation) designed to help students construct knowledge about some aspect of phenomena. Teachers can use the planning activity to initiate learning cycle lessons by thinking through the types of hands-on activities that allow students to make an accurate scientific claim. Our ideas about planning learning cycle instruction are consistent with the approach used to teach about planning 5E models and constructivist learning theories (see Brown 2018). Teachers should pinpoint some aspect of the desired content that students can explore. Remember, the goal is to provide an experience where students construct an accurate understanding from evidence and then connect all other knowledge to it. Thus, the most critical planning for the learning cycle is at the overlap of two learning cycle phases—exploration and concept introduction.

The juncture of the exploration and concept introduction is when students construct knowledge based on firsthand experiences. It is vital that students have explorations that produce valid and reliable evidence, and in turn, allow students to explain scientific phenomena at a conceptual level. Teachers should teach students about the importance of being objective and think about patterns in data and causal relationships during hands-on investigations. Students should formalize their ideas through writing, discussions, and other presentations. Teachers must carefully select an activity based on the goals of the lesson and overall unit of study. For example, in Chapter 7, "Students' Use of the PSOE Model to Understand Weather and Climate," a key goal for student learning was to get them to have experiences where they could create a claim about energy transferring in only one way. We carefully picked a demonstration that allowed for multiple variations to illustrate that thermal energy transfers in one direction, from hot to cold objects. At the end of the demonstration, students wrote an evidence-based claim. Remember, the research shows that when students learn new content, exploring science before explaining new ideas is superior to other instructional sequences.

Once teachers have designed the exploration that produces accurate understanding, they can plan other activities to make more robust learning experiences for students. Teachers should keep in mind that the scholarship shows that all of the phases of the learning cycle are necessary because each plays an essential role in learning (Abraham 1992). For example, teachers can develop didactic forms of instruction (lectures and readings) aimed at explaining the rationale or scientific principles and co-constructing a reasoning statement with students. Teachers can think through how they want to introduce new terms and concepts that are not easily invented or necessary to discover firsthand. Students can practice new ideas in similar and different contexts to form deeper understanding.

Having a solid exploration-concept introduction also can seamlessly lead to activities that can motivate student interest in science learning at the onset of a unit. Adding an *engage* phase aligns with the cognitive science research and the 5E instructional model (Bybee et al. 2006) If teachers are using demonstrations, discrepant events, or an experiment as explorations, they can have students make predictions about some aspect of the phenomena to gain student interest and elicit prior knowledge. Then, students can conduct investigations to explore the scientific ideas and collect quantitate or quantitative data.

Finally, having a well-conceived exploration-concept introduction plan of activities leads to the concept application phase. Students can have extended learning by carrying out additional demonstrations or investigations to develop an understanding that is more sophisticated and to test ideas in a new and different situation. Teachers can easily add evaluation phase activities so students can self-reflect on their learning and so teachers can provide a summative assessment of student learning. Adding an *evaluate* phase aligns with the 5E model that is based on the learning cycle and cognitive science research (Bybee et al. 2006)

The Sequence of Instruction Conclusions

How we sequence science instruction has powerful implications for learning. The research on the learning cycle is quite clear that explore-before-explain instructional sequences are optimal for learning, and each phase is vital for developing students' intellectual growth. While sequence science instruction in a learning cycle, 5E, or PSOE is a goal, teachers should keep in mind that developing this ability might take some time. We have found that a first step in creating learning cycle activities can best be accomplished by taking a tried-and-true, hands-on exploration that you are currently using and placing it first in your instructional sequence. We have also learned that while planning learning cycle sequences of instruction may take more time upfront, teachers gain back this time because they do not have to reteach as much content or process skills. Teachers are pleasantly surprised that the learning cycle promotes long-lasting understanding and students retain ideas because their own firsthand experiences support them. The learning cycle is just one approach we have successfully used to promote evidence-based inquiry. Next, we will share an approach that can be used on its own or in a learning cycle sequence to engage students and promote deeper conceptual understanding.

Further Reading

Abraham, M.R. 1992. Instructional strategies designed to teach science. In *Research matters . . . To the science teacher*, eds. F. Lawrenz, K. Cochran, J. Krajcik, and P. Simpson (pp. 41–50.). Manhattan, KS: NARST Monograph #5.

Abraham, M.R., and J.W. Renner. 1986. The sequence of learning cycle activities in high school chemistry. *Journal of Research in Science Teaching*, 23, 21–43.

Atkin, J.M., and R. Karplus. 1962. Discover or invention? *The Science Teacher*, 29, 45–47.

Bransford, J., A. Brown, and R. Cocking. 2000. *How people learn: Brain, mind, experience, and school*. Washington, DC: National Academy Press.

Brown, P. 2018. *Instructional sequence matters: Structuring lessons with the NGSS in mind*. Arlington, VA: National Science Teachers Association Press.

Bybee, R.W. 1997. *Achieving scientific literacy: From purposes to practices*. Portsmouth, NH: Heinemann Educational Books, Inc.

Bybee, R.W., J.A. Taylor, A. Gardner, P. Van Scotter, J.C. Powell, A. Westbrook, and N. Landes. 2006. *The BSCS 5E instructional model: Origins, effectiveness, and applications*. Colorado Springs: BSCS. www.bscs.org/curriculumdevelopment/features/bscs5es.html

Karplus, R., and H.D. Their. 1967. *A new look at elementary school science*. Chicago, IL: Rand McNally.

Purser, R.K., and J.W. Renner. 1983. Results of two tenth-grade biology teaching procedures. *Science Education*, 67, 85–98.

Renner, J.W., M.R. Abraham, and H.H. Birnie. 1988. The necessity of each phase of the learning cycle in teaching high school physics. *Journal of Research in Science Teaching*, 25, 39–58.

Shymansky, J., W. Kyle, and J. Alport. 1983. The effects of new science curricula on student performance. *Journal of Research in Science Teaching*, 20(5), 387–404.

3

Using Classroom Inquiry as a Pathway to Evidence-Driven Science Activities

Patrick Brown and James Concannon

An evidence-based inquiry is an approach where students seamlessly learn science content and the nature by which scientific knowledge is produced in valid and reliable ways. The nature by which scientific knowledge is produced has long been a vital learning standard for some time. The practices of how scientific knowledge is developed have been termed "inquiry" and described by the National Research Council (NRC 2000) to consist of five essential features.

1. The learner engages in scientifically oriented questions.
2. The learner gives priority to evidence.
3. The learner formulates explanations based on evidence.
4. The learner connects explanations to scientific knowledge.
5. The learner communicates and justifies explanations.

Each of the essential features of classroom inquiry varies on a continuum according to the amount of self-direction offered to the student and the degree to which the teacher or materials provide guidance. For example, consider essential feature 1, "learner engages in scientifically oriented questions." Depending on students' prior content knowledge and abilities to do science, teachers can choose to engage students in a question they (or the materials) provide, let students select from possible questions, or have students pose their unique question. Each of the remaining essential features of classroom inquiry varies in the same way from being teacher directed to student led. Thus, using the essential features of classroom inquiry allows for a whole host of implementation possibilities directly related to students' prior knowledge and experiences. Remember, a major theme that came up in the research chapter related to cognition and learning is that students' prior knowledge serves as the foundation for building accurate understanding.

Secondly, classroom inquiry can fluctuate from being full to partial. A full inquiry includes all of the essential features of classroom inquiry, while a partial experience includes any number fewer than all five essential features. There is only one condition where an activity is not inquiry based—when the experience includes no essential features. The importance of this attribute of classroom inquiry cannot be overstated. Classroom inquiry is very flexible, so teachers can use the essential features to address almost all the content they teach. The key is that teachers understand how the essential features can vary to accommodate learning goals and include a plethora of possibilities for instructional practice.

The research on inquiry is quite expansive, and studies have investigated science teachers' implementation of essential features of inquiry into instruction, students learning science in an inquiry-based classroom, and students learning about scientific inquiry (Lederman and Niess 2001). Regarding the scholarship on teachers' views of inquiry, some studies show that they have difficulty embracing inquiry because they hold a limited view that does not align with a more research-based perspective consisting of five essential features. These individuals conceive of inquiry teaching as only an entirely student-directed, independent approach (Brown, Abell, Demir, and Schmidt 2006).

The research findings demonstrate that students are motivated in an inquiry classroom because the instruction is relevant, transferable, and useful in future problem-solving situations (Anderson 1997). In addition, research advocates developing students' inquiry skills at an early age so they have the abilities to use their observations and data to make inferences and evidence-based claims (Harlen 2001). Inquiry improves students' attitudes and student achievement and helps close the gender, ethnic, and socioeconomic status gap concerning science achievement (Freedman 1997; Von Secker and Lissitz 1999).

Planning Tips for Classroom Inquiry Teaching

In Cothron, Giese, and Rezba's (1989) book *Students and Research*, the authors suggest using questioning strategies to help students develop their scientific experiments vs. giving students specific directions. While our strategy draws on Cothron and colleagues' work aimed at helping students construct investigations with guidance, our approach is unique. We start with what we call the planning wheel and use it to structure the investigation. The planning wheel can be an advanced organizer worksheet for students, a diagram on the board, a poster that is used to structure thinking, or a conceptual framework for promoting conversations about creating an inquiry investigation. The planning wheel is analogous to a Ferris wheel and consists of three main parts that include the central hub, spokes, and passenger cars (see the figure of a planning wheel used in the model lesson in Chapter 6). Like an experiment that includes many variables that interact and have causal relationships, each part of a Ferris wheel has a role while also being dependent on one another.

We use the central hub and ask students to think about a specific aspect of some phenomena. Our goal is to get students to think about how something works or acts in natural instances. We do not have one standard guiding question that works in all instances, and teachers will have to think about the learning goals for the lesson and the desired content they want students to investigate. Also, teachers should keep in mind that this stage of instruction is guided. We use students' natural inquisitiveness and the desired content to arrive at a feature, an aspect, or some action that occurs and can eventually be tested within the confines of our classroom or school and uses readily available materials. Teachers should assess students' prior knowledge and experience with the content at hand.

The next stage is dedicated to designing the investigation. We ask students what factors influence what they have written in the central hub. Students list the factors they come up with as the spokes in the inquiry-planning wheel. Students can easily do this on their own, in groups, or as a whole class activity. The point is for students to generate a list of all of the factors they can think of that influence the phenomena under study.

What the inquiry-planning wheel so nicely orchestrates for students is the relationship between different variables in an investigation. Once the factors are listed, it is time to decide what will be the primary variable explored in the investigation. We have students choose the factor they want to test in the exploration. We also ask students whether they can change more than one factor at the same time and know exactly how the change affects the central hub. The chosen spoke becomes the independent variable, the center of the planning wheel is the dependent variable, and all other spokes are constants in an investigation. Whether teachers introduce these terms at this grade level or address them on a conceptual level is up to them.

Combining the independent and dependent variables from the planning wheel allows students to form research questions for investigation. Keep in mind that while planning an inquiry investigation may take some time, studies show that inquiry improves students' attitudes and student achievement. Also, using the planning wheel addresses the first essential feature of inquiry and meets our goal of engaging students in scientifically oriented questions (NRC 2000)

Fair Test Issues

We follow up the inquiry-planning wheel with discussing fair test issues that will be necessary to seek answers to our research question. We focus on brainstorming a set of instructions for carrying out the investigation that will allow for accurate results. Thinking through the variables and their relationships as well as the fair test helps students begin to conduct investigations. Discussing fair test issues is a way to bridge students' investigatory questions with the explanations they form and begins to address the second essential feature of inquiry that students give priority to evidence when responding to questions (NRC 2000). Also, research shows that helping students carry out their investigations makes the experiences considerably more intellectually challenging and motivating.

Next Step Investigations

The inquiry-planning wheel opens up a whole host of possibilities for follow-up investigations. A logical complement and extension to students' guided experiences using the inquiry-planning wheel is to open up explorations so they are more student-centered in what we call *next step investigations*. The key to a next step investigation is not so much to develop content knowledge per se but to allow the student the chance to demonstrate knowledge and abilities to self-direct their inquiry investigation. We revisit the planning wheel and have students choose a different variable to test on their own. Students complete a very similar process as the guided and full inquiry on their own in a more-open, self-directed format. The next step investigation allows students to apply problem-solving strategies in similar and different contexts. Again, the research shows a tremendous intellectual benefit for students who gain knowledge and skills from conducting more open inquiry investigations. The ultimate goal is that students start to learn to use the principles of classroom inquiry to construct knowledge on their own about a phenomenon that interests them.

Inquiry Conclusions

Giving students ownership for the learning plays a vital role in heightening their motivation and helping them self-monitor their developing understanding. Research on inquiry shows that it improves student's conceptual understandings and helps them understand science knowledge as well as science practices as a valid and reliable way to generate new knowledge. Thinking about classroom inquiry as varying from student to teacher directed and including essential features allows for a whole host of implementation options. Teachers can easily implement partial or full classroom inquiry in nearly every activity that involves hands-on data collection. When we place inquiry-based teaching in a learning cycle sequence, we can heighten learning even more by placing primacy on student's firsthand experiences before teacher explanations. In the next section, we will discuss our third and final pathway to evidence-based science activities that can be used on its own or in combination with classroom inquiry and explore-before-explain teaching.

Further Reading

Anderson, O.R. 1997. A neurocognitive perspective on current learning theory and science instructional strategies. *Science Education*, *81*(1), 67–89.

Brown, P., S. Abell, A. Demir, and F. Schmidt. 2006. College science teachers' views of classroom inquiry. *Science Education*, *90*(5), 784–802.

Cothron, J.H., R.N. Giese, and R.J. Rezba. 1989. *Students and research: Practical strategies for science classrooms and competitions* (2nd ed.). Dubuque, IA: Kendall/Hunt.

Freedman, M. 1997. Relationship among laboratory instruction, attitude toward science, and achievement in science knowledge. *Journal of Research in Science Teaching*, *34*(4), 343–357.

Harlen, W. 2001. *Primary science . . . taking the plunge: How to teach primary science more effectively for ages 5 to 12*. Portsmouth, NH: Heinemann Educational Books, Inc.

Lederman, N.G., and M.L. Niess. 2001. An attempt to anchor our moving targets. *School Science and Mathematics, 101*(2), 50–57.

National Research Council. 2000. *Inquiry and the national science education standards.* Washington, DC: The National Academies Press.

Von Secker, C., and R. Lissitz. 1999. Estimating the impact of instructional practices on student achievement in science. *Journal of Research in Science Teaching,* 36(10), 1110–1126.

4

Using Phenomenon-Based Teaching as a Pathway to Evidence-Driven Science Activities

Patrick Brown and James Concannon

The idea of phenomenon-based learning has a long history in education. Ancient philosophers had questions about natural occurrences and sought evidence and used logical thinking to explain the underlying principles and mechanisms. Phenomenon-based teaching is an extension on the early thinking habitats of philosophers and emphasizes the critical role that questioning and deep engagement in exploring a natural phenomenon play in learning.

The idea behind phenomenon-based teaching is to focus students' experiential learning on science experiences that lead to wonderment about the natural world. Beneficial explorations invoke curiosity and promote investigations that produce empirical data of qualitative observation and accurate, evidence-based claims. Phenomena are observable events about which we can use scientific knowledge and abilities to develop a deeper conceptual understanding. Meaningful science phenomena for science lessons are complex entities that are best understood through multiple learning experiences (e.g., explorations, lectures, readings, discussions) and allow other key, associated ideas to be easily connected to students' experiences. Science phenomena are not factoids and are essential because they contextualize all science learning during a topic of study.

Phenomenon-based teaching is a constructivist based approach. Research supports phenomenon-based learning in science education, and the cognitive sciences that suggest instruction should begin by motivating and enticing students' intellectual abilities while also identifying prior knowledge (Bransford, Brown, and Cocking 2000). Because phenomenon-based teaching is such an expansive approach, it can be included under many different headings including "project-based" and "problem-based." According to Krajcik and his colleagues, the following characteristics are beneficial ways to motivate kids in phenomenon-based activities:

1. A driving question that engages students in investigating an authentic problem or situation
2. Collaborative learning around the phenomena under study
3. Technology appropriate to the problem
4. Products that represent what students have learned (Krajcik, Blumenfeld, and Berger 2002)

Research in these areas shows that using authentic and meaningful contexts that phenomenon-based teaching provides engages students in developing deep conceptual understanding (Brown and Abell 2007). Contextualizing learning by focusing on phenomena helps students not only learn science content but also helps them create scientific hypothesis and variables in an experiment (Rivet and Krajcik 2004). Veermans and Jarvela (2004) found that focusing on phenomena to guide learning helps students form evidence-based claims that answer the driving question. The situation of learning around phenomena also increases student motivation. Zumbach, Kumpf, and Koch (2004) found that students who were engaged in a relevant phenomenon to learn had higher motivation than students who learned similar content in a traditional setting. Phenomenon-based approaches anchor learning in real world, natural occurrences, and the knowledge and skills gained can be used across subject areas and science disciplines.

Planning Tips for Classroom Phenomenon-Based Teaching

We have found that the key to phenomenon-based teaching is to find learning experiences that can be guided by a driving question, lead to hands-on, minds-on exploration that produces data and evidence, and allow students to make evidence-based claims, and encourage students to create artifacts that demonstrate their science knowledge. The driving question is essential and should address something that is meaningful and important to learners. The driving question is critical in meeting the other key components of phenomenon-based learning. The driving question sets up the explorations that students will have that provide them with data and evidence, and in turn, allows them to construct a more in-depth understanding.

Because the driving question is of utmost importance, it deserves further exploration. Implementing a driving question is an art and should both address students' misconceptions and engagement wonderment in some natural occurrence. There are many ways to find important phenomena to drive lessons. Students' misconceptions result from students' lack of personal experience or are due to deeply rooted conceptual misunderstandings. Many of the books mentioned before by Keeley and colleagues on student misconceptions provide excellent insight into typical student misconceptions, and therefore, meaningful phenomena to explore (see the further reading section in Chapter 1).

We have included numerous examples of using phenomena to situate and motivate learning in our model lessons. For example, in Chapter 8, "Two-Liter Bottles and Botanical Gardens: Using Inquiry to Learn Ecology," students are engaged in a multiweek exploration of life and the interdependence of organisms. The driving question that situates and motivates learning is how students can create a self-sustaining ecosystem using specific components similar to those found on Earth. Students engage in multiple explorations to collect data; they conduct library research and receive some direct instruction about the content. Students create an artifact and give presentations—a poster presentation of their ecosystem that explains the interdependence of organisms. The poster presentation is a culminating project to assess student learning and for students to reflect on their developing understanding. The bottled ecosystem is an excellent example of phenomenon-based learning experience that includes a driving question, data collection, student collaboration, and the construction of an artifact to demonstrate learning. In addition, the bottled ecosystem model lesson is also an example of how phenomenon-based teaching can overlap with both the learning cycle because the lesson is designed in a 5E sequence and classroom inquiry because the lesson includes all five essential features of classroom inquiry.

Conclusions

Phenomenon-based teaching is a multidisciplinary approach that situates learning in meaningful contexts. The key behind a phenomenon-based approach to instructional design is to target natural occurrences that interest students and brainstorm driving questions related to the situation. Once students have driving questions, they can determine individually or collaboratively the best way to investigate the phenomena to gain deeper conceptual understanding. In this way, phenomenon-based teaching works well on its own or easily integrates with the other research-based pathways described so far. What many find is that the pathways naturally intersect and that the design principles associated with one directly relate to all pathways.

So far we have described seminal science research for students and its implications for teaching. We have also provided guidance for using three research-based pathways to learning—the learning cycle sequence of instruction, classroom inquiry, and phenomenon-based teaching. Each of the pathways has been significant themes in *Ready, Set, Science! Putting Research to Work in K–8 Science Classrooms* (Michaels, Shouse, and Schweingruber 2008). Although students' background experiences vary from child to child, using the pathways as core approaches to science teaching is a highly effective approach to develop all kids' knowledge. We have one more topic to explore before illustrating how the pathways can be used to teach third- through fifth-grade students in science effectively. We want to show teachers how the three research-based pathways naturally translate into the practices outline in *A Framework for K–12 Science Education: Practices, Crosscutting Concepts, and Core Ideas* and the *Next Generation Science Standards* (NGSS Lead States 2013; NRC 2012)

Further Reading

Bransford, J., A. Brown, and R. Cocking. 2000. *How people learn: Brain, mind, experience, and school*. Washington, DC: The National Academies Press.

Brown, P., and S. Abell. 2007. Project-based science and the elementary classroom. *Science and Children*, 45(4), 60–61.

Krajcik, J., P. Blumenfeld, and C.F. Berger. 2002. *Teaching science in elementary and middle school classroom: A project-based approach*. New York: McGraw Hill.

Michaels, S., A.W. Shouse, and H.A. Schweingruber. 2008. *Ready, set, science! Putting research to work in K-8 science classrooms*. Board on Science Education, Center for Education, Division of Behavioral and Social Science and Education. Washington,

DC: The National Academies Press. www.nap.edu/catalog/11882/ready-set-science-putting-research-to-work-in-k-8#toc

National Research Council. 2012. *A framework for K-12 science education: Practices, crosscutting concepts, and core ideas. Committee on a conceptual framework for new K-12 science education standards*. Board on Science Education, Division of Behavioral and Social Sciences and Education. Washington, DC: The National Academies Press.

NGSS Lead States. 2013. *Next generation science standards: For states, by states*. Washington, DC: The National Academies Press. www.nextgenscience.org/next-generation-sciencestandards

Rivet, A.E., and J.S. Krajcik. 2004. Achieving standards in urban systemic reform: An example of a sixth-grade project-based science curriculum. *Journal of Research in Science Teaching*, 41(7), 669–692.

Veermans, M., and S. Jarvela. 2004. Generalized achievement goals and situational coping in inquiry learning. *Instructional Science*, 32(4), 269–291.

Zumbach, J., D. Kumpf, and S.C. Koch. 2004. Using multimedia to enhance problem-based learning in elementary schools. *Information Technology in Childhood Education Annual*, 25–37.

5

Connecting to Contemporary National Science Standards

Patrick Brown and James Concannon

As many veteran teachers know, with time comes educational change. The release of the Next Generation Science Standards (NGSS) raised many questions for teachers like, How are the new standards going to change my teaching? How do I convert the new standards into practice? While the new standards reflect advancement in the science education community, we have found using one or more of the three pathways previously described in daily classroom activities allows for the seamless translation of the NGSS into practice. Using the pathways opens opportunities for teachers to address the three interconnected dimensions of NGSS: Science and Engineering Practices, Crosscutting Concepts, and Disciplinary Core Ideas (NGSS Lead States 2013; NRC 2012).

Practices, Crosscutting Concepts, and Disciplinary Core Ideas for K–12 Curriculum

Practices
The eight essential science and engineering practices embody the vision for what students should know and be able to do to understand about the world they live in (summarized in Bybee 2012). The revision, in part,

reflects the difficulty teachers had embracing "inquiry-based" teaching due to misconceptions between what "inquiry" means in teaching and everyday vernacular (Bybee 2012). Similar to the essential features of inquiry, the eight science and engineering practices (SEP) can vary from being teacher- to student-directed for a range of implementation strategies. The practices are overlapping, meaning asking questions leads to designing and conducting experiments, and then making sense of observations derived from experiences with data and evidence.

Crosscutting Concepts

The crosscutting concepts (CCC) have explanatory power across the science and help bridge the SEPs with the Disciplinary Core Ideas. The CCC are common themes in science and useful for explaining science and science as a way of knowing (summarized in Duschl 2012). For example, students can use observed "patterns" and "cause and effect" to bridge their experiences with data to an evidence-based claim. In this example, pattern recognition in data and seeking to understand the mechanisms behind cause and effect are logical thinking tools that help students understand the natural world in much the same way that scientists carry out their work. Thus, the CCCs are embedded in the SEPs and content under study.

Disciplinary Core Ideas

The final dimension is the one most familiar to teachers and is the content. The Disciplinary Core Ideas (DCIs) include key ideas in major science fields (e.g., Earth and space science, physical science, life science). Also, the nature of science and engineering technology is included as DCIs. Each of the DCIs includes component ideas that offer more specific information related to content standards (see Table 5.1).

Connecting the Three Pathways to the NGSS

It is helpful to expand our view of effective teaching when translating the NGSS into classroom instruction. The "pathways" to evidence-based inquiry and the anatomy of the standards are closely connected (teachers may find it helpful to go back and forth between this section and Table 5.1). For instance, consider how the explore-before-explain instructional sequence connection to the NGSS. Many explorations ask students to investigate scientific questions (alignment with SEPs 1 and 3). Students' explorations produce data that requires analysis (alignment with SEP 4).

Table 5.1 The Three-Dimensional Frameworks

Science and Engineering Practices	Crosscutting concepts
1. Asking questions (for science) and defining problems (for engineering)	1. Patterns
2. Developing and using models	2. Cause and effect: Mechanism and explanation
3. Planning and carrying out investigations	3. Scale, proportion, and quantity
4. Analyzing and interpreting data	4. Systems and system models
5. Using mathematics and computational thinking	5. Energy and matter: Flows, cycles, and conservation
6. Constructing explanations (for science) and designing solutions (for engineering)	6. Structure and function
7. Engaging in argument from evidence	7. Stability and change
8. Obtaining, evaluating, and communicating Information	

DCIs

Physical Science
- MS-PS1 Matter and its Interactions
- MS-PS2 Motion and Stability: Forces and Interactions
- MS-PS3 Energy
- MS-PS4 Waves and Their Applications in Technologies for Information Transfer

Life Science
- MS-LS1 From Molecules to Organisms: Structures and Processes
- MS-LS2 Ecosystems: Interactions, Energy, and Dynamics
- MS-LS3 Heredity: Inheritance and Variation of Traits
- MS-LS4 Biological Evolution: Unity and Diversity

Earth and Space Science
- MS-ESS1 Earth's Place in the Universe
- MS-ESS2 Earth's Systems
- MS-ESS3 Earth and Human Activity

Engineering, Technology, and Applications in Science
- MS-ETS1 Engineering Design

According to the data collected, what students think about patterns, trends, and cause and effect relationships (all CCC) can help students make evidence-based claims (alignment with SEP 6). Students evidence-based claims should be about science content that is either directly related to or an elaboration of the curriculum (alignment with DCIs). These are just a few of the easy ways the explore-before-explain sequence translates to the NGSS.

A similar transition to NGSS occurs when teachers use an "inquiry" pathway in their classroom. Consider the essential features of inquiry

1 and 2 that explain that learners should "engage in scientifically oriented questions" and "give priority to evidence." By engaging students in scientifically oriented questions, teachers are covering many SEPS (alignment with 1, 3, 4, and 5). In addition, similar to the explore-before-explain sequence, CCCs are embedded in the "inquiry" activity as a necessary part of the data analysis. When teachers ask students to "connect explanations to scientific knowledge" and "communicate and justify explanation," they are engaging student in the SEPs 6, 7, and 8. In sum, inquiry directly translates to NGSS dimensions in many ways.

Finally, phenomenon-based approaches also directly relate to the NGSS. A critical aspect of phenomenon-based teaching is investigating science to form deep conceptual understanding. If students' investigations are hands-on that produce data, they would be engaging in many potential SEPs and CCCs. Also, the "theme" or phenomena of interest should relate to a teachers' curriculum, and therefore, be related to DCIs. Teachers who home in on meaningful and relevant topics that require hands-on exploration open up the inclusion of all three dimensions of the NGSS.

Meaningful Professional Development

Few activities are more potent than the reflection on practice. We have noticed that educators learn best when they have opportunities to collaborate, have active learning experiences, and can focus on student learning. The model lessons that follow serve as great reflective tools for teachers to develop a deeper understanding of the NGSS in practice. While NGSS documents provide an extensive overview of the infrastructure of the integration of SEPs, CCCs, and DCIs, the model lessons provide examples of how to put the vision of the standards into practice.

We have success teaching educators how to unpack standards by using the model lessons that illustrate the three dimensions of the framework. Teachers, professional developers, science educators, and curriculum teams can carry out active professional learning by implementing the model lessons with students and then reflecting on practice.

One of the most beneficial activities educators can do is reflect on teaching and create NGSS "connection" tables (see Table 5.2 as an example). NGSS connection tables allow teachers to align activities used in the model lessons with their corresponding dimensions of the NGSS. Teachers have learned quite a bit about their practice from connecting the model lessons to the NGSS. Some teachers who use the pathways are validated that their existing practices align with the NGSS. For others, the

Table 5.2 Connecting to the Next Generation Science Standards (NGSS Lead States 2013)

3-PS2–1 Motion and Stability: Forces and Interactions
www.nextgenscience.org/pe/3-ps2-1-motion-and-stability-forces-and-interactions

Performance Expectation	Specific Connections to Classroom Activity
Plan and investigate to provide evidence of the effects of balanced and unbalanced forces on the motion of an object.	Students work in groups to create a paper helicopter, they predict how fast the helicopter will travel in seconds, and they describe the forces acting on a paper airplane.
	During the evaluation phase students design a new and unique helicopter given a set of parameters and a specific problem scenario.

Lesson Level Performance Expectation (LLPE)

LLPE 1: Plan an investigation to provide evidence that the change in an object's motion depends on the sum of the forces on the object.	During the exploration phase students focus on force to determine how changing the size of a paper helicopter influences flight.
LLPE 3: Develop and use a model to show how forces interact in a system of study to produce motion	Students use force diagrams to show how forces with different magnitudes and directs can be used to describe motion in a system of study.

Science and Engineering Practices

Asking questions and defining problems	Students investigated whether the size and mass of paper helicopters influences how fast they travel
Developing and Using Models	Students learn how to use force diagrams as a model for describing how many different forces interact and whether the interaction among forces results in motion.
Planning and carrying out investigations	Students developed a procedure based on observations of helicopter flight.
Using mathematical and computational thinking	Students calculate means from raw data to look for patterns
Constructing explanations from evidence	Students make evidence-based claims about the relationship between helicopter size and flight
Engaging in argument from evidence Obtaining, evaluating, and communicating information	Students' helicopter conclusions make a Claims-Evidence-Reasoning (C-E-R) statement from data they have obtained firsthand

Targeted Disciplinary Core Idea

PS2.A: Forces and Motion Each force acts on one particular object and has both strength and a direction. An object at rest typically has multiple forces acting on it, but they add to give zero net force on the object. Forces that do not sum to zero can cause changes in the object's speed or direction of motion. (Boundary: Qualitative and conceptual, but not a quantitative addition of forces are used at this level.)	Students use force diagrams to describe that paper helicopters experience a gravitational force pulling them toward the ground. Some students realized that paper helicopters also experience the force of air resistance on the blades.

Connections to the Nature of Science

Scientific Investigations Use a Variety of Methods Science investigations use a variety of methods, tools, and techniques.	Students' experiences using the inquiry-planning wheel help them understand how to design a valid and reliable investigation. Each unique investigation will require a specific experimental design.

"pathways" provide a more research-based structure for creating lessons and curriculum. Regardless, having teachers connect standards to model lessons is the type of activity that gives them purpose and intention for three-dimensional understanding learning. Learning is similar for students and teachers. Just like students benefiting from learning science that is relevant to their lives, the model lessons contextualize the NGSS for instructional practice.

Translating a Model Lesson to the NGSS

This model lesson puts a new spin on a classic investigation involving paper helicopters (See NGSS connection table 5.2). Students design and carry out investigations to learn about forces and interactions. Students engage in three-dimensional learning to explore the relationship between force and motion that uses principles of explore-before-explain teaching and essential features of classroom inquiry. The culminating activity asks students to create a model as a solution to a problem and innovate, if necessary, to improve the design. There are numerous chances for formative assessments so they can scaffold learning activities to build students' knowledge and many chances for students to reflect on their developing understanding. This model lesson lends itself to developing more coherent curriculums that connect ideas from physical sciences

Conclusions

The importance of teachers connecting the model lessons and the NGSS is a major theme of this book. The hard work of translating the model lessons to the NGSS is a powerful professional development strategy that takes teachers' practice to new levels. Many teachers have commented that using the model lessons and reflecting on the connection to the NGSS has helped teach them quite a bit about learners and learning and about instructional strategies that can improve student achievement and motivation and has deepened their content knowledge. The result is that teachers have developed their ability to translate the NGSS into practice and know how to approach instructional design from a more pedagogical perspective.

Further Reading

Bybee, R. 2012. Scientific and engineering practices in K-12 classrooms: Understanding a framework for K-12 science education. *The Science Teacher*, *78*(9), 34–40.

Duschl, R.A. 2012. The second dimension—crosscutting concepts. *The Science Teacher*, 79(2), 34–38.

National Research Council. 2012. *A framework for K-12 science education: Practices, crosscutting concepts, and core ideas. Committee on a conceptual framework for new K-12 science education standards*. Board on Science Education, Division of Behavioral and Social Sciences and Education. Washington, DC: The National Academies Press.

NGSS Lead States. 2013. *Next generation science standards: For states, by states*. Washington, DC: The National Academies Press. www.nextgenscience.org/next-generation-sciencestandards.

6

Engage Students in Designing Experiments so Hands-on Science Does Not Spiral Out of Control

Patrick Brown

I have success engaging fourth- and fifth-grade students in a student-centered investigation of forces and interactions. The lesson builds on students' prior knowledge and highlights three-dimensional learning (Science and Engineering Practices, Disciplinary Core Content, and Crosscutting concepts) to address the Performance Expectation (PE) that students should be able to "plan and conduct an investigation to provide evidence of the effects of balanced and unbalanced forces on the motion of an object" (3-PS2–1) (NGSS Lead States 2013). The lesson that follows is a powerful way to share the responsibility for learning between teacher and student, and student and to set high expectations of "doing science" for the rest of the school year.

Day 1 (Approximately 30 Minutes)

I start by having students make predictions about how long it might take a paper helicopter to travel from the ceiling to the floor. Students have varying conceptions, but most believe it will take between 1 and 5 seconds.

I follow up the conversation by introducing the investigation planning wheel to students (see Figure 6.1). The planning wheel is a way to prompt student thinking about essential factors in an experiment so they can design and conduct more valid and reliable investigations. I tell students that we are going to place "time it takes a helicopter to fall to the ground" in the center of the wheel. Next, we brainstorm possible factors that might influence how fast helicopters fly and list them as the spokes of the wheel. Students generated a flurry of ideas that included but were not limited to: size of the helicopter, a mass attached to the helicopter, the material helicopter is made from, the shape of the blades, and size of the body.

The planning wheel almost became an intellectual challenge for students who want to see how many different possible factors they can come up with that influence helicopter fall time. At this point in the lesson, we decide which factor we wanted to test as our first investigation. After some debate, the student consensus was to test whether the mass of the helicopter influences helicopter speed. We also discussed whether we could change another listed factor at the same time as we changed the size. Students quickly realized that once we decided on what we would change, the remaining ideas should stay the same throughout the investigation.

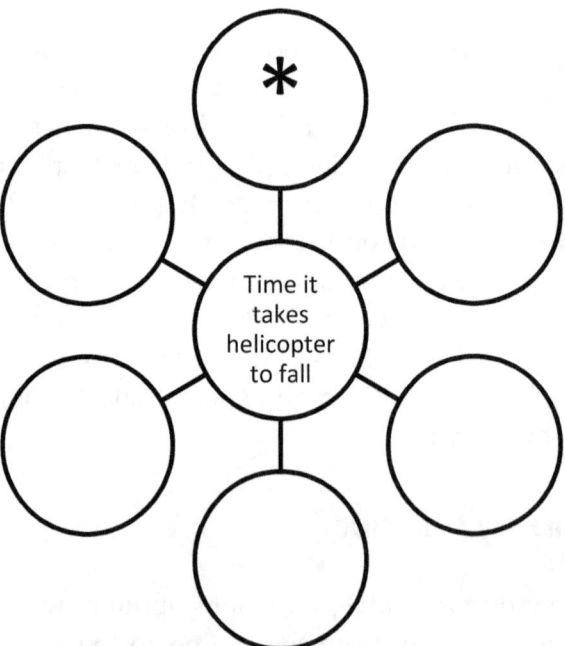

Figure 6.1 Investigation Planning Wheel

We would revisit the planning wheel during subsequent days to design and carry out other related activities.

The last activity of the day was to have students predict which helicopter would hit the ground the fastest and to label the forces acting on the different paper helicopters. We planned to drop the helicopters in the stairwell of our school. Students had a variety of ideas, and there was no clear class "winner" regarding a predominating view of the fastest helicopter. Students also had varying conceptions of the forces acting on a helicopter. Nearly all students identified a force pulling the helicopter to the ground and that the helicopters had different masses. Also, some students realized that the force of air resistance (i.e., "drag") would act in the opposite direction of gravity. Students were less sure about the relationship between the magnitude of these forces and how forces may be different when comparing helicopters of different masses. I learned that students did not have a clear sense of how they could model the forces acting on an object using force diagrams.

Day 2 (45 Minutes)

The second day's activities were dedicated to students collecting quantitative data on their helicopters. I provided some procedural support when students had a question and had them work in groups of three (recorder, dropper, and timer). Many questions emerged as students began to conduct their initial tests. Many of students' questions were answered with further questions. For example:

Student Question: "Do we have to drop the helicopters from the same height?"
Teacher Answer: "How would changing the height you dropped each helicopter influence your results?"
Student Question: "Do we just drop each helicopter one time?"
Teacher Answer: "How many times do you think you need to drop each helicopter to get accurate results?"

I wanted the investigation to be about students "doing science" in a way that was logical and not focused on giving them precise directions and affirming their ideas. Although I tried to guide them through probing questions, there was quite a bit of learning through trial and error about how to experiment. Although students were unconformable without

Table 6.1 The Relationship Between Mass and Paper Helicopter Fall Time

Number of Paper Clips	Helicopter Fall Time			
	Trial 1	Trial 2	Trial 3	Mean*
1	4.7	4.5	4.5	4.6
2	6.4	6.8	6.5	6.5
3	7.1	7.1	7.0	7.1
4	7.8	7.8	8.0	7.9
5	10.1	10.4	8.9	9.8
6	10.4	10.6	10.0	10.3
7	12.5	10.6	10.9	11.3
8	12.5	11.4	11.4	11.7

*Note: Calculating the mean or average was beyond the math curriculum, and I helped students calculate

having a standard procedure to follow, they quickly learned that their role was to collect data and start to think logically about trends, patterns, and relationships. As students performed their explorations and observed patterns in their data, they became more confident that their approach was reliable and they could conduct their investigations (see Table 6.1 for representative student data).

Many students commented that the investigation was more straightforward to perform than first anticipated. For instance, they realized the importance of controlling as many factors to ensure accurate results after seeing variations in their data due to error. Students also noticed that one trial for each helicopter would not give them accurate results; however, ten or more trials for each helicopter mass were also unnecessary. At the end of the exploration, I was pleased that students focused on data collection and developing their abilities as scientists. I was also glad to see students used logical thinking skills to make sense of their data when looking for patterns (i.e., crosscutting concept). Once I started noticing students thinking about what data meant, we transitioned to the explanation.

Day 3 (Approximately 25 Minutes)

Students were ready to start to make evidence-based claims, so we delved directly into the content being explored. First, students made an evidence-based claim that the mass of the helicopter influences the time it takes to fall. I also asked students to compare their data with their initial prediction as a way for them to think about their knowledge and developing understanding. I wanted students to go beyond their evidence-based claim to describe the scientific principles involved in the investigation (termed a "reasoning" or "warrant" statement). We would add the reasoning statement to students' claims based on evidence later in the explanation phase.

We revisited students' force diagrams to help bridge their experiences with a more in-depth understanding of how forces influence motion (This was our lesson level performance expectation). Students needed some technical instruction on how to represent a system of study using force arrows. Students' force diagrams were a way of teaching model-based reasoning because their diagrams would both explain and help them make predictions about a system of study. I showed them that the length of an arrow indicates the magnitude and the way the arrow points shows the direction. When students looked at their initial ideas about the forces involved with helicopters, they realized that "weight" force and air resistance (i.e., "drag") forces act in opposite directions and were not equal in magnitude. What this meant is that students need to represent the "weight" forces acting on the helicopter with longer arrows that pointed in the opposite direction as the air resistance ("drag"). Students also were able to get much more specific in their force diagrams and think regarding cause and effect (e.g., a crosscutting concept). Thus, the model helped students write a reasoning statement to explain to students that unbalanced forces cause motion.

I had students combine their evidence-based claims with their scientific reasoning statements (Claims-Evidence-Reasoning [C-E-R]) as a way to have them record their knowledge and understanding. Student's C-E-R statements were a nice interdisciplinary bridge to English Language Arts (ELA) and the Common Core Standards (CCSS) that suggest that students should be able to "Provide a conclusion statement or section that follows from and supports the information or explanation presented" (National Governors Association Center for Best Practices [NGA] and Council of Chief State School Officers [CCSSO] 2010). Students' C-E-R statements set the stage for a seamless transition to the next set of investigations.

Day 2 (Approximately 15 Minutes) and Day 3 (Approximately 30 Minutes)

During the elaboration, we revisited the investigation planning wheel to see what other factors we could explore to learn more about paper helicopters. I wanted students to build their knowledge to promote deeper

Table 6.2 Influence of Helicopter Size on Fall Time

Paper Helicopter Size	Helicopter Fall Time (seconds)			
	Trial 1	Trial 2	Trial 3	Mean
Small	8.4	8.2	7.9	8.2
Medium	4.7	4.5	4.5	4.6
Large	2.9	2.7	2.7	2.8

understanding. As a class, we decided that paper helicopter size would be an excellent factor to test.

Because students had worked out the details and fine-tuned their procedure for testing helicopters in the explore phase, they could efficiently conduct this "next step" investigation in a short amount of time. They learned that the different helicopters had slightly different masses (small = 0.3g; medium, 1.3g; and large 1.8g) that would influence their fall time but also had different blade lengths. Students focused on differences in the blades of the helicopter and noted in their diagrams that bigger blades meant more surface area in contact with air, and therefore, greater forces when in contact with the air. Students worked in groups to model the forces involved with helicopters of different sizes.

After students explained the scientific principles, they conducted their tests. Their data was strong support for their force diagrams and effect of increasing helicopter size on fall time (see Table 6.2).

Day 3 (Approximately 30 Minutes) and Day 4 (Approximately 30 Minutes)

As a closing activity, I wanted to see whether students had developed scientific abilities and knowledge of the relationship between forces and mass on the motion of an object. I challenged students to design a helicopter with a different size and mass than we tested and one that would fall at precisely 2.0 seconds given a specific flight distance. My evaluation was an engineering task, and students had to design a solution to a problem and generate iterative testing so they could redesign and perfect their model. I had students draw their prototype including their labeled force diagram (summative assessment) before they conducted tests. In addition, students performed force calculations for their chosen mass. The end product of their testing and my summative evaluation of their learning was for them to complete a laboratory write-up with their data, an explanation of how close they came to accomplishing the task, and a claims-evidence-reasoning statement (summative assessment).

Conclusions

An artfully crafted explore-before-explain lesson aids teachers in bundling the three dimensions of the frameworks into useful lessons so students can transfer ideas to develop more in-depth understanding. Students enjoyed the helicopter investigation and their abilities to do science, and knowledge of force, mass, and motion were long-lasting because they were based on their firsthand experiences. The paper helicopter investigation is a great way to start the school year and directly relates to other physics topics, allowing for bundling of PEs, to promote transfer of knowledge and learning. This force and motion lessons can quickly be followed up with an exploration of energy transformation where students can connect ideas about potential energy and kinetic energy to their helicopter data. In this way, the paper helicopter lessons help sets the stage for a more coherent curriculum, where topics in each physics unit are connected and revisited throughout the semester.

References

National Governors Association Center for Best Practices & Council of Chief State School Officers (NGA/CCSSO). 2010. *The common core state standards for English language arts & literacy in history/social studies, science, and technical subjects. Appendix A: Research supporting key element of the standards.* Washington, DC: Author.

NGSS Lead States. 2013. *Next generation science standards: For states, by states.* Washington, DC: The National Academies Press. www.nextgenscience.org/next-generation-sciencestandards (accessed July 14, 2016).

7

Students Use of the PSOE Model to Understand Weather and Climate

Patrick Brown and James Concannon

A thoughtfully sequenced Earth and space science demonstration can be fundamental to helping students formulate, revise, and develop ideas to promote long-lasting understanding. We have success teaching sixth-grade students using an exploration-before-explanation instructional sequence called the PSOE model that consists of the following phases: predict, share, observe, and explain (Haysom and Bowen 2010; Stepans 1996). The PSOE instructional sequence is a useful tool for designing science lessons because it helps teachers focus on essential concepts and highlights that students learn best when they are actively engaged in thinking and doing and have the chance to build new ideas before teacher explanations (Bybee 1997).

We derived the investigation using Stepan's (1996) description of the phases and purposes of the POE model to include the three-dimensional nature of the K–12 Frameworks (seamless integration of essential science practices, crosscutting concepts, and disciplinary core content). Weather and climate are highlighted in the Next Generation Science Standards. The lesson centers around the PE (performance expectation) that asserts that students should "make observations to provide evidence that energy can be transferred from place to place by sound, light, heat, and electric currents" (4-PS3–2) (NGSS Lead States 2013). Understanding the relationship between "cold" and "hot" substances and thermal energy transfer is important for understanding how fluids interact in the air (some weather phenomenon) and water (ocean currents). We use what we term "molecular talk" during discussions to bridge students' observations of science on the macroscopic level with a microscopic explanation of weather and ocean currents.

The lesson that follows is a quick and cost-effective way to prompt sixth-grade student thinking about the mechanism behind weather patterns.

Demonstrations 1 and 2: Hot Water Set Into Cold Water, Cold Water Set Into Hot Water (Seven Minutes)

We have students predict (predict phase) what happens in two different set-ups (see Figures 7.3 and 7.4). In the first set-up, hot water (65°C) is placed in a 50 ml Erlenmeyer flask and colored red. Then, students are told that the flask will be submerged into a 900 ml beaker filled with cold (9°C) water. The second set-up is the exact opposite: students are told that the 50 ml flask with cold water (9°C) dyed blue will be placed in a 900 ml beaker with hot water (65° C). (Note: The food coloring allows students to identify the differences in the temperatures of water. We decided to dye only the water in the flask in each scenario so that it was easier to see when changes occurred.) After telling students the scenarios, we have them draw on paper their predictions for both scenarios to show what will happen to the water in the flasks after being submerged into the beaker (see Figures 7.1 and 7.2 for students' predictions).

Next, during the share phase, students talk through their ideas with a partner. Students' sharing included all likely possibilities. Some students thought that in both set-ups the dyed water (red or blue) would move out of the flask into the beaker of water. Other students believed that only the red-colored or blue-colored water would move into the beaker of water. A few students thought that nothing would happen and neither of the colors of water (red or blue) would move. During this time, students asked each other questions, requested evidence for claims, and explained their thinking using logical reasoning. To our surprise, some students discussed that they thought water could move in only one direction in each set-up (from the flask to the beaker), reasoning that water could move only into the beaker because the flask was already full. The concept that water could

Figure 7.1 Student Prediction for the Transfer of Thermal Energy From "Hot" to "Cold"

Figure 7.2 Student Prediction for the Transfer of Thermal Energy

only move one way became a very appealing idea for the class, which led to performing an additional demonstration (see Demonstration 3). (See Figures 7.1 and 7.2 for student predictions.)

Teachers should remain "active" listeners during the discussion, encourage student-to-student conversations, and not focus on correct answers. Our encouragement during the share phase was aimed at motivating students to talk through their ideas and not at whether they had accurate conceptions.

Once all the students had shared their ideas, it was time to have them *observe* what would happen when two different temperatures of water were allowed to come in contact with each other. The food coloring was pivotal for promoting conceptual understanding and provided the visual support for students to be able to explain the phenomenon. First, we put the 50 ml flask containing hot water (65°C) dyed red in the 900 ml beaker containing cold water (9°C). The red-colored water quickly moved in a steady stream into the surrounding cold water (9°C). Students said that the first set-up looked like a "volcano exploding" (see Figure 7.3).

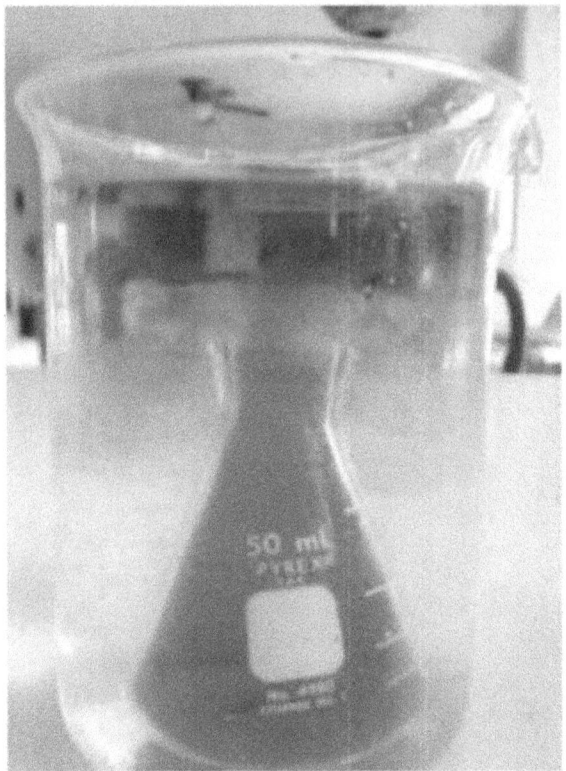

Figure 7.3 Picture of the Transfer of the Thermal Energy from "Hot" to "Cold"

Next, we placed the cold (9°C) dyed water in the 50 ml flask into the 900 ml beaker containing hot water (65°C). To students' surprise, the cold water did not move into the warm water in a steady stream (see Figure 7.4). In fact, more than a minute after the flask had been placed in the beaker, the cold water still had not moved into the beaker.

At the end of the observe phase, students drew their observations. Students observed that the water moved from hot to cold in the first set-up. Also, students witnessed that the cold water did not move into the surrounding hot water (see Figure 7.5). Students' observations were not graded but helped them construct evidence-based claims that occurred later in the lesson.

Demonstration 3: Hot Water Set Into the Cold Water

We had not anticipated the idea that water could move in only one direction—from the flask to the beaker—and students determined we needed to test another set-up. In the third set-up, we filled a flask with hot water (65° C)

Figure 7.4 Picture of "Cold" Water Dyed Blue Not Moving Into Less Dense, "Hot" Water

Figure 7.5 Student Drawing and Explanation of "Cold" Water Dyed Blue Not Moving Into Less Dense, "Hot" Water

and placed it in a beaker filled with cold water dyed blue. Some students were surprised by the results when we placed the hot water (65° C) in the flask into the cold blue water (9°C) in the beaker. After a minute, we removed the flask from the beaker and the students observed cold water slowly moving in a steady stream to the bottom of the flask. As one student explained, the steady stream looked like a "reverse volcano."

Discussion: Connecting Key Concepts and Introducing New Terms

Teachers can tap into children's innate curiosity to help them develop more complex thinking skills in which firsthand science experiences serve as the foundation for deeper learning. The skill of asking kids to make connections between firsthand experiences and science content is an important step in developing conceptual understanding and can be facilitated through purposeful and focused investigations. The missing information needed to help develop students' understanding of some weather phenomena was related to the density and molecular motion of "hot" versus "cold" water. Thus, once students explained their observation, we challenged them to make a scientific claim about the hot vs. cold water, the interactions that take place when hot and cold materials come in contact with each other, and to propose a mechanism for which some large air masses and water masses move on Earth. The explanation following the exploration was a way for students to develop a deeper conceptual understanding by anchoring new ideas with their firsthand experiences and observations. Also, the evidenced-based claims are a way for students to use model-based reasoning (i.e., crosscutting concept) to explain a phenomenon (weather and ocean currents) that is not readily observable firsthand.

We had students write claim statements about the density of hot and cold water based on observations. For example, students wrote for their evidence-based claim that, "The hot water looked like a cloud on top of the cold water." Another student explained that the cold water "dropped to the bottom" and looked like a "steady flowing blue stream of water."

We learned that even though we had students make evidenced-based claims, not all students have a scientific understanding of the phenomena under study. As a result, our students benefited from what we term "molecular talk," where we compare the molecules in "hot" vs. "cold" water material of the same volume. We used our fingertips to represent water molecules and moved them at different speeds to represent the different energy between hot and cold molecules. Thus, students were able to explain the evidence (e.g., "hot" water dyed red floats and "cold" water dyed blue sinks) that supports the claim (hot water has more thermal energy than cold water). Thus, we meet the goal that students understand the DCI that states, "energy can be moved from place to place by moving objects or through sound, light, or electric currents" (PS3.A: Definitions of Energy, NGSS Lead States 2013).

The most challenging part of students' evidence-based claims is proposing a mechanism for which large air masses or water masses interact over time. Students can relate what they observed firsthand with the hot and cold water demonstrations to weather. Students reason that the Earth's atmosphere and oceans are made up of different air masses or water masses with varying temperatures (prior knowledge) that interact. For example, when air masses or water masses with different temperatures collide, the colder air mass or water mass sinks below, the warmer air or water mass. The different color water demonstrations provide visual support for the interaction of air masses and represent the interaction of air or water masses as a result of the interaction of different temperatures. In this way, students were beginning to learn how scientists can use patterns to explain and make predictions about the weather (NGSS Lead States 2013).

The explain phase was also a chance for students to derive concepts and new terminology from firsthand experiences. For example, we called the movement where cold surface water sinks below the warmer underlying water "convection." By introducing new formal terminology and concepts in light of students' firsthand experiences with a visual model, we maintained high levels of engagement during discussions, and students were able to attach meanings to these new ideas.

Conclusions

We found that these activities increased our interests and helped them learn about convection currents in water and air. Although convection demonstrations have been performed by many teachers for a long time (see Roth n.d.), the use of the PSOE demonstration was an exciting way to promote scientific understanding and reasoning to propose explanations for challenging content (Haysom and Bowen 2010; Stepans 1996). Using different colored waters has many applications for teaching process and interactions. The concept of convection can be used to explain many Earth and space science concepts that will be taught in middle and high school such as: (1) mantle convection playing an essential role in plate tectonics; (2) formation of cumulus clouds and thunderstorms; and (3) separation between layers in Earth's (and other planetary) atmospheres. In addition, having students describe their understanding of the demonstration and discussion through writing helps prepare them for advanced science topics and develops their thinking and acting like scientists (supporting and proposing ideas through writing). Most importantly, the exploration-before-explanation sequence promotes deep conceptual understanding because new ideas and concepts are based on students' firsthand experiences with data and evidence.

References

Bybee, R.W. 1997. *Achieving scientific literacy: From purposes to practices.* Portsmouth, NH: Heinemann Educational Books, Inc.

Haysom, J., and M. Bowen. 2010. *Predict, observe, explain: Activities enhancing student understanding.* Arlington, VA: National Science Teachers Association Press.

NGSS Lead States. 2013. *Next generation science standards: For states, by states.* Washington, DC: The National Academies Press. www.nextgenscience.org/next-generation-science-standards (accessed September 28, 2015).

Roth, J. n.d. *Lesson plan: Hot, cold, fresh, and salty. NOAA ocean service education, lesson plan library.* http://oceanservice.noaa.gov/education/lessons/hot_cold_lesson.html (accessed June 28, 2015).

Stepans, J. 1996. *Targeting student's science misconceptions: Physical science concepts using the conceptual change approach.* Riverview, FL: Idea Factory Inc.

8

Two-Liter Bottles and Botanical Gardens

Using Inquiry to Learn Ecology

*Patrick Brown, Patricia Friedrichsen,
and Lou Mongler*

Just outside the high school's door is a premier location to showcase nature's wonders. We use our immediate biological world and engage students in designing 2L-bottle ecosystems. The simple inquiry activities in this project increase student motivation while addressing several national standards. The national standards include that students develop the ability to "construct an argument that plants and animals have internal and external structures that function to support survival, growth, behavior, and reproduction" (4-LS1–1), and ("use models to describe that energy in animals' food used for body repair, growth, motion, and to maintain body warmth) was once energy from the sun" (5-PS3–1) (NGSS Lead States). We describe this project using a 5E instructional model of inquiry learning that includes (1) engagement, (2) exploration, (3) explanation, (4) elaboration, and (5) evaluation (Bybee 2002).

Engagement

On the first day of the unit, we entice students with a "life or death" challenge: to design a self-sustaining ecosystem that can survive for three weeks. We call our projects *mini-ecosystems*. Because the weather in the midwestern United States is pleasant in the early fall, students eagerly go outside to explore nature through this hands-on investigation. The following criteria and guiding questions help students design their mini-ecosystems and help us assess students' prior knowledge.

Mini-Ecosystem Criteria:
- Must contain aquatic and terrestrial components
- Should include four organisms (no vertebrates)
- One organism must be a plant

Students usually want to know whether their entire grade for the project is dependent on their organisms staying alive for the duration of the three weeks. Many students ask, "How will our organisms get food and water if we seal our mini-ecosystems and do not put in additional foods?" Others want to know, "How will our insects get oxygen if the bottles are airtight?" Although technically the mini-ecosystems are not 100% airtight—a small amount of gases and water move in and out—they serve as models to discuss many different types of self-sustaining systems and cycles in an ecosystem. We use the following guiding questions with students:

1. What will be the oxygen source in your mini-ecosystem?
2. What will be the carbon dioxide source in your mini-ecosystem?
3. How will plants and animals obtain water?
4. What will serve as food sources for the organisms in your mini-ecosystem?

We use one 50-minute class period to collect organisms, but, given student excitement, this is barely enough time. Adjacent to our school is a large pond, and we take a field trip to the pond to collect organisms. For many students, the challenge is so alluring that they search outside of school time with their friends for unusual specimens. If an outside source of organisms is not readily available, inexpensive materials such as elodea, snails, soils, and seeds can be purchased. We check students' designs to ensure that appropriate organisms are used; students are not allowed to use vertebrates such as small mammals or fish.

When it is time to build the mini-ecosystems, we share examples of models from the book *Bottle Biology* (Ingram 1993) and investigate real-life contained systems such as the Biosphere II Project. We encourage students to be creative when designing their mini-ecosystems, and, because each system must contain linked aquatic and terrestrial components, students have to draw on their knowledge of the water cycle and the oxygen-carbon dioxide cycle before beginning.

Some students use two bottles attached one on top of the other. First, they create an aquatic environment with pond water in the bottom bottle and cut off the top of the bottle that has the spout. Next, they connect an inverted 2L bottle to serve as a terrestrial habitat on top. They use the bottle cap as a filter by poking small holes to allow for the transfer of water but not terrestrial components. These types of systems are similar to the ones laid out for students in *Bottle Biology* (Ingram 1993).

We have been pleasantly surprised that many students use creativity to fabricate complex bottle systems. For instance, we have had successful four-bottle mini-ecosystems that contain two terrestrial and two aquatic habitats. Students who create these types of mini-ecosystems connect the bottles so they lie flat and form the outline of a square. Making students design their systems allows us to assess their prior knowledge about the interdependence of organisms. We reinforce proper safety procedures by having them wear goggles, aprons, and gloves and help students cut the bottles.

Exploration

Students marvel at the mini-ecosystems they design and line up at the door before school to check their ecosystems. After the initial construction stage, we give students 15 minutes of class time each day to make observations and ask questions about their mini-ecosystems. For many students, this is a nature-based reality television program: worms and pill bugs are active, rustling through the dead leaves and soil, spiders build webs, and grasshoppers jump from twig to twig. Like the outdoors, our mini-ecosystems do not allow anyone to edit out real-life events: death touches students.

Explanation

After building and observing their mini-ecosystems, students can use evidence from the exploration activity to explain new concepts. We ask students to draw a scale image of their mini-ecosystem to illustrate numerous cycles that occur there. For instance, students draw arrows showing that oxygen produced by plants cycles to the animal life, and carbon dioxide produced by animals cycles to plant life. Students answer the following guiding questions:

1. From where do plants get energy?
2. How are all the organisms in a habitat interconnected?

The mini-ecosystem mimics a real, natural system while allowing students to control variables such as animal and plant life. The guiding questions thus encourage students to use their observations of the mini-ecosystem to explain how biological systems work at the most basic level. We find that students have the most difficulty explaining food webs. Library research on their organisms can help students make sense of their observations and construct food webs of their ecosystems.

Elaboration

Because many students are excited about their mini-ecosystems, we capture this enthusiasm to extend learning to real ecosystems. Students learn about food webs, the carbon-oxygen cycle, and the water cycle in more complex systems. Some students will discover through their library research that not all food webs display predator-prey interactions.

Evaluation

As teachers, we enjoy the activities in the evaluation phase because we use student presentations as an alternative form of assessment. Students summarize their understanding of ecology through a poster presentation at our mini-ecosystem research symposium. During our symposium, students use evidence from their mini-ecosystems to demonstrate their content knowledge and question each other about the interactions that occurred in their systems. Students like to learn about their classmates' mini-ecosystems and whether their selected organisms survived the three-week project. The presentations are an excellent chance for students to communicate their understandings of ecology gained through the use of scientific inquiry of their mini-ecosystems (NRC 1996).

To give our students a wider audience, we ask them to display their posters in our teachers' lounge. This aspect of the project provides an opportunity for other faculty members to see how three weeks of inquiry learning come together in a formal, culminating project. We find that many faculty members want to know more about using a 5E lesson to motivate students and that many students talk about the project in other classes. Students enjoy an extra sense of reward from the feedback they receive from other teachers.

Conclusions

Using a 5E instructional model helps us design inquiry experiences for our students and motivates our students to learn ecology. Students get involved as they make daily observations, take measurements, answer guiding questions, and create models of their ecosystems. Using these hands-on guided activities at the beginning of the year gets students excited about science for subsequent units. In the future, we plan to extend the elaboration phase of this project to include school-wide conservation efforts and to raise community awareness of recycling and pollution issues.

Although our ecology unit is at the beginning of the school year, the spring would also be an excellent time to collect organisms and build mini-ecosystems. By letting students create their mini-ecosystems, we allow them to develop a personal interest in the interactions present in their models. As a result, they learn fundamental ecology concepts through this inquiry approach.

References

Bybee, R., ed. 2002. *Learning science and the science of learning.* Arlington, VA: National Science Teachers Association Press.
Ingram, M. 1993. *Bottle biology.* Dubuque, IA: Kendall/Hunt.
National Research Council. 1996. *National science education standards.* Washington, DC: The National Academies Press.

9

Enhancing Elementary Students' Experiences Learning About Circuits Using an Exploration-Explanation Instructional Sequence

Patrick Brown and Tim Brown

One highly effective strategy to helping elementary students make sense of abstract concepts is to sequence instruction so students have hands-on opportunities to investigate science before being introduced to new science explanations (Brown and Abell 2007). Students need to place new ideas in a framework for understanding that only firsthand experiences provide. Fourth-grade teachers can design units on circuits to follow an exploration-explanation instructional sequence so they can confront student's misconceptions and help them build an accurate understanding of science. This article provides elementary teachers with a student-centered sequence of science instruction that emphasizes the NGSS PE that states, "Make observations to provide evidence that energy can be transferred from place to place by sound, light, heat, and electric currents" (4-PS3–2).

Exploration

The driving question that engages students in the lesson is, "Using the fewest number of materials, how can we light a bulb?" First, students draw out their predictions. Their ideas typically include the misconception that set-ups that do not form a complete loop will light a bulb. For example, they think that no matter where a wire is connected to a battery and a bulb, a complete circuit is made (see Figure 9.1). Next, all of the students' predicted set-ups are collected and posted on the front board. In groups of two, students explore all the alternative set-ups using the materials mentioned in the following list. Underneath the posted pictures, students collect data about whether each set-up was successful in lighting the bulb.

Materials
- One AA battery (Use only non-rechargeable batteries. Rechargeable nickel-cadmium batteries could cause instant burns.)
- One flashlight bulb
- Wire

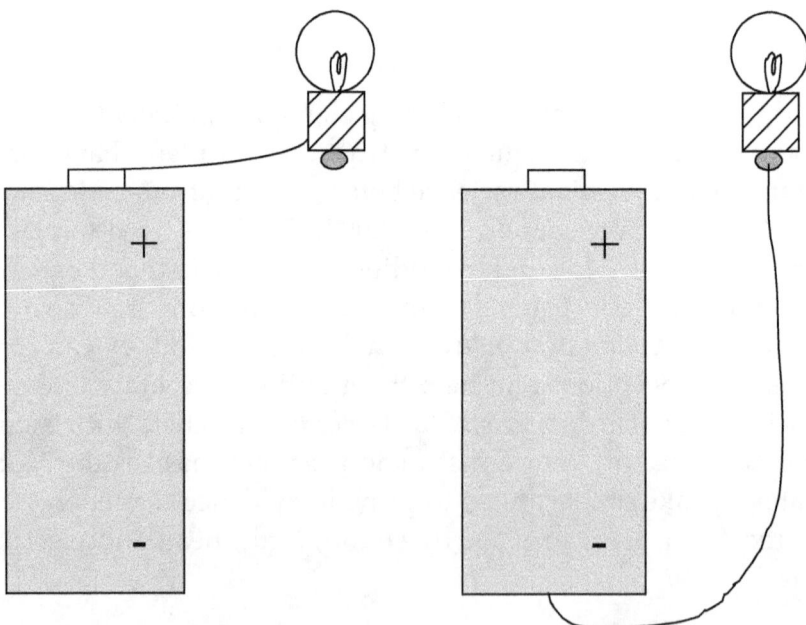

Figure 9.1 Incomplete Circuits Because Wire Does Not Form a Complete Loop

Safety

- Teachers should be aware that set-ups that create a short circuit can make the wires hot (e.g., see set-up in Figure 9.2).
- Students should wear safety goggles when working with glass light bulbs and wire.

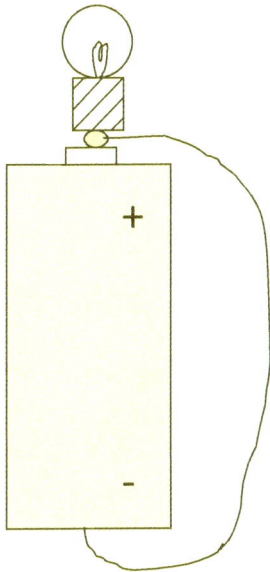

Figure 9.2 Short Circuit Because Wire Does Not Touch Screw Threads

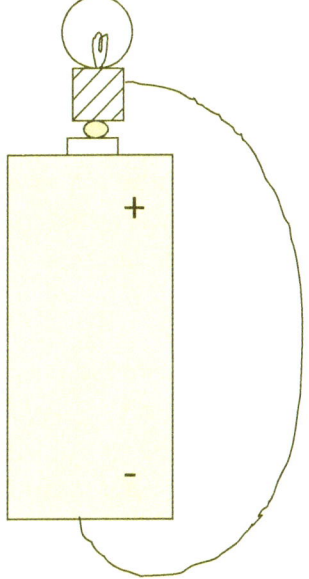

Figure 9.3 Bulb Lights Because It Is Part of a Complete Loop

It is crucial at this point in the lesson for students to explain the phenomena in their own words before the teacher introduces new terms. What students can explain is that wires, batteries, and bulbs must form a complete loop to light the bulb. Additionally, many students did not know about the importance of the screw threads as points of contact that are necessary to light the bulb. From the exploration activities, students can determine that the screw threads on a light bulb are essential in making a complete loop (see Figure 9.3). These activities highlight the importance of students formulating explanations from evidence to answer scientifically oriented questions and serve as the transition to the explanation phase of instruction.

Explanation

Interactive Discussions

An interactive discussion is a strategy that engages students' prior ideas and uses activities, embedded formative assessments, and peer sharing to relate new content to experiences. The focus of interactive discussions is on meaningful teacher-student interactions and students self-monitoring their understanding through frequent assessments—not on students copying notes. This interactive discussion includes: (1) a checkpoint for understanding questions; (2) new terms; (3) self-tests; (4) analogies; and (5) exit slip assessment.

Checkpoint for Understanding
The purpose of the checkpoint is for students to commit to their ideas and self-monitor their learning. Individually, students writing down on an index card what they learned from the exploration activities (i.e., which set-ups light the bulb) and what they are still confused about after investigating wires, batteries, and light bulbs.

New Terms
As a large group, students identify different components of a circuit. These include: (1) source of the energy—the battery; (2) the desired object—the light bulb; (3) the contact point on the light bulb—the screw threads; and (4) the connectors—the wires. Additionally, students look at the difference between the two terminals at each end of the battery (i.e., one positive and one negative terminal). Once students have identified these components, the teacher can discuss with students that circuits in series are used to

describe the type of circuit they have been investigating. Circuits in series form a complete electrical loop from the negative end of the battery, to the contact points (screw threads) on the source (light bulb), and back to the positive end, using wires. Thus, the new terminology, the term "series," is developed in light of students' prior experiences.

Self-Test
Following the introduction of the term "series," students practice new ideas using a "self-test." The purpose of a self-test is to allow students to check their understanding of new content and terminology individually. During the self-test, students explain whether different diagrams containing wires, light bulbs, and a battery form a complete loop and are a circuit in series.

Analogies
Teachers can summarize the lesson by discussing that a circuit in series is like riding a bike. For example, legs turning the pedals on a bicycle are like a battery and the back bicycle tire is like a light bulb. Students finish the analogy by explaining that the chain is like the wire that forms the complete loop. Students relate to the analogy and explain that circuits in series are like riding a bike—both need a complete connection between all of the components to work correctly.

Exit Slips
At the end of the lesson, students go back to their "checkpoint" index card and answer their initial question. Their answers serve as the "exit slip" to get out of class and a way for the teacher to assess whether students understand the concepts. Many times students can answer their questions if they were confused about how to use a battery, light bulb, and a wire to make a circuit in series. Other times, students' initial questions lead to subsequent explorations in the unit such as investigations of parallel circuits and conductors and insulators. For example, students typically want to know whether two batteries will light a bulb, whether one battery and multiple wires can light two bulbs, and whether all types of wires that are metal will work to light the bulb.

Conclusions

The results of this exploration-explanation sequence help students understand circuits in series. Providing experiences before terminology offers a way for teachers to promote critical thinking because students challenge their existing conceptions and carry out meaningful investigations to test their ideas. In subsequent lessons on circuits (e.g., circuits in parallel and using different types of resistors like fans and motors) students can brainstorm possible investigative questions so they can ask and seek answers to their scientific questions—an essential feature of scientific inquiry (NRC 2000).

Switching the explain-explore sequence to provide firsthand experiences for students upfront creates the need for teachers to move beyond traditional paper-pencil activities and focus on student learning and active participation at all phases of instruction. Although switching the sequence takes no more time than traditional lessons (this lesson took two days), the first step is putting the exploration activities at the beginning of the lesson. Then, teachers can incorporate formative assessments like "checkpoints," "self-tests," and "exit slips," into explanations. Teachers will find that students understand the concepts better when hands-on activities are followed by explanations that are interactive and include discussions, frequent assessments, and writing. While this strategy might present some challenges, its advantages are that it helps to cultivate critical thinking skills that are necessary for learning science.

References

Brown, P., and S. Abell. 2007. Examining the learning cycle. *Science and Children*, 44(5), 58–59.

National Research Council. 2000. *Inquiry and the national science education standards*. Washington, DC: The National Academies Press.

10

Elementary Students' Investigations in Natural Selection

Nancy Bartley, James Concannon, and Patrick Brown

Elementary students love learning about how animals behave, what animals eat, why some animals are more dangerous than others are, and why animals look the way they do. This lesson taps into this natural curiosity and ignites students' curiosity about camouflage and mimicry! The goal for this third grade lesson is for students to demonstrate an understanding of the advantages of being camouflaged, how animals become camouflaged, and why some animals mimic more dangerous organisms (National Science Education Standard, Life Science Content Standard C: Organisms and their Environments [National Research Council [NRC] 1996]; A Framework for K–12 Science Education, Dimension Three, Core Ideas: LS3.B [NRC 2012]; and Next Generation Science Standards, Variation of Traits: LS3.B [NRC 2013]). Our experience teaching this lesson is that students believe animals such as lions and zebras (animals that do not automatically change color like the chameleon) had at one point in their ancestry mindfully changed colors to blend into their environment. Students have said, "Owls look like trees because that is where they live." Students cannot articulate that resulting from competition and predator/prey interactions, specific physical and behavioral characteristics within a population of a particular species are more beneficial for survival and, subsequently, more likely to reproduce. At the end of the lesson, students should understand that rather than animal selection, it is the environment selecting certain physical or behavioral traits over others.

Theoretical Framework: The 5E Constructivist Model of Learning

This lesson is unique from others of its kind (Collins 2010; Josephs 2011) in that it follows the 5E (Engage, Explore, Explain, Elaborate, and Evaluate) constructivist model with explicit steps, questions, and considerations to implement guided inquiry using inexpensive and easy-to-find materials. The 5E instructional model was developed by the Biological Sciences Curriculum Study as an aid for teachers to foster inquiry and conceptual change (Bybee 1997). By following the 5E Constructivist Learning Model, teachers can set the stage for students to consider their initial ideas and questions (Engage); carry out initial investigations and collect evidence (Explore); and, finally, communicate evidence and explanations (Explain). A formal explanation is provided after students have time to gather and process evidence and, subsequently, consider prior ideas in light of new evidence.

Teachers can approach the implementation of the 5E model anywhere along the inquiry continuum from "open" to "guided" (NRC 2000). A guided inquiry occurs when information is provided to the students, such as providing a scientifically oriented/testable question, a procedure, and the variables students need to collect. On the other hand, open inquiry occurs when students develop their own scientifically oriented questions, procedures, variables, and method for data analysis (NRC 2000).

Materials

- Several pieces of colored paper (at least four separate colors)
- A hole puncher to make dots from the paper
- Ziploc bags (one per student)
- Four small Dixie cups
- Stopwatch or timer
- Glue sticks
- Poster board
- Marker
- Scissors
- White computer paper
- Access to a computer lab and the Internet

Preparation

Start with four different colors of several pieces of computer paper (for example, yellow, green, pink, and blue). For a class of 20 students, use the hole puncher to make a minimum of 480 small paper circles (dots)—120 dots for each of the four colors. Separate the dots by color by placing them into four different Dixie cups. Each Dixie cup should have 120 dots. Next, get out the Ziploc bags.

Each student will need a Ziploc bag, so for a class of 20 students, 20 bags are required. Place five dots of each color into each Ziploc bag (Figure 10.1). Each bag should contain five yellow, five green, five pink, and five blue dots for a total of 20 dots per bag. The Ziploc bags are used for the explore phase of the lesson. In each Dixie cup, there should still be 20 dots of each color. The 20 dots remaining in each color are used for the first activity of the Engage phase.

Day 1

Engage Phase (7–10 Min)

Begin this lesson by projecting pictures from the computer of camouflaged animals living in their environments. Pictures of a lion camouflaged in the savanna, a gray owl in a tree, a tiger in the jungle, a deer in tall grass, a

Figure 10.1 Ziploc Bag With 20 Dots (Color Figure Available Online)

praying mantis on a leaf, and a leafy sea dragon are found relatively easily on the Internet. To add relevance to the lesson, teachers can mention that when the gray owl and deer appear, that they live near our homes.

Ask, "Did you see the animals? Where these animals difficult to see? Why was it difficult to see the animals?" It might be easier for students to see the animals in some of the pictures, but not all. It is important to pause (wait time) between each question. Students will explain that these animals are more difficult to see since they are camouflaged.

Explore Phase (40 Min)

The Explore phase consists of two activities intended to introduce to students the idea that some animals in a population have better odds of survival from predation because these animals exhibit specific characteristics, that being color, and that some characteristics are favored as a result of environmental pressures. The first activity is merely a demonstration involving only a few students to ensure the class understands how to do the second activity of the Explore phase.

For the first activity, create a scenario whereby students act as a predator, specifically hawks, trying to pick up as many mice in the environment. The environment is a simple piece of colored paper, and the prey—the mice—are dots of paper scattered on the environment. Show the class four pieces of paper (yellow, green, pink, and blue), and ask for four volunteers to act as predators. Each volunteer should stand in front of one piece of colored paper. Explain that in this activity, students are "hawks" and that the piece of paper is the environment. Then, give each volunteer a Dixie cup filled with 20 colored dots all of the same color, but of a color that does not match the color of their papers. For example, a student standing in front of a pink piece of paper could have 20 blue dots. Instruct the student to dump out his or her cup and spread the dots out over the paper (Figure 10.2). The dots represent mice, and the colored paper represents the environment.

Ready, set, go—start the timer. Students race to find out how many mice they can pick up, one at a time, in 10 seconds. Students frantically pick up as many dots as they can! After the fun 10 seconds, have students count their dots to determine who won. Say, "That was easy, wasn't it? Why was it so easy? What would have made it harder?" From our experience, students explain it was rather easy and realize that it would have been harder had the dots been the same color as the paper.

Students immediately get excited when we say, "That was a simple demonstration of what you will all be doing! Each of you will be a hawk!"

Figure 10.2 A Pink Paper With Blue Dots Used for the Demonstration (Color Figure Available Online)

Figure 10.3 A Student Recording Results; on the Yellow Paper, She Left Four Yellow Dots (Color Figure Available Online)

For each student, pass out the data collection tables (Figure 10.3), a single piece of colored paper, and a Ziploc bag of containing 20 dots (Figure 10.1). Just as before, everyone in the class is going to get a chance to be the "hawk," but part of it will be a little different in that the mice are different

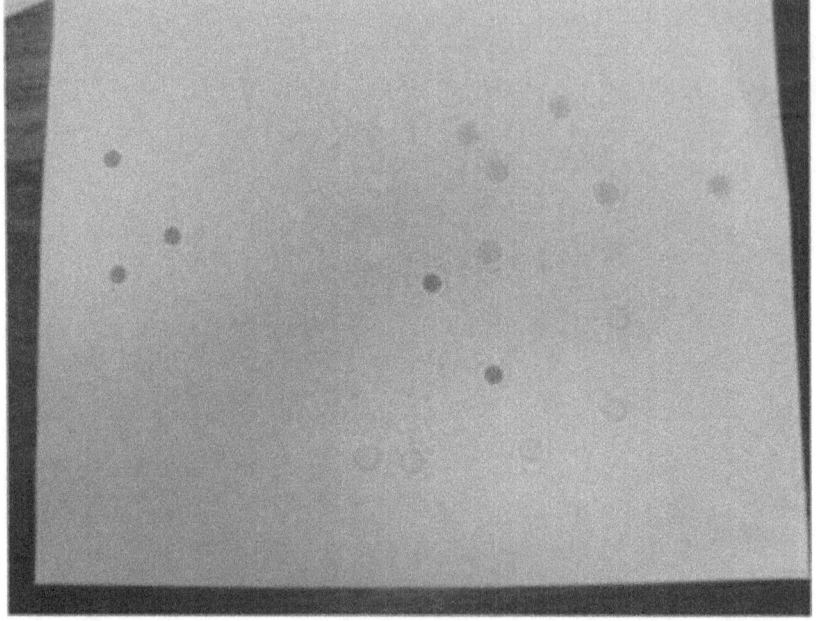

Figure 10.4 A Pink Environment With Five Mice of Each Color (Color Figure Available Online)

colors. To help prevent students from picking up only one color (say only blue dots on a blue paper), preface the activity by saying:

> Hawks in nature are not picky; their primary objective is to find food as fast as they can so they do not have to spend a long time and extra energy hunting. So, to be a hawk, you cannot be picky about what color mice to pick up. You have to pick up the dots that are easiest to get.

Note to Teacher

In general, students pick up fewer dots of the same color as the environment, but not always. Sometimes, but not too often, students pick up the same number of camouflaged dots as other colored ones. Because of this, it is critical for each student to carry out three trials, record their results from each trial, and take an average. The three trials altogether take about 20 min. At the end of the trials, students need to individually answer the follow-up questions either on the back or a separate sheet of paper (Appendix A).

To begin the activity, have students place the paper on their desks and mix their dots all around. Students have 10 seconds to pick up the dots, and the dots have to be picked up one at a time. After the 10 seconds, students record their results. On average, students pick up just one or two dots of the same color as the paper "environment."

Day 2

Explain Phase

The essence of the Explain phase is for students to process their data and to explain their findings. Begin the second day of the lesson by giving students time to analyze their data and to create an explanation for their findings. Students share and discuss their results in the follow-up section of the handout (Appendix A) with their neighbors. This is a quick and effective means for students to compare results and to determine if others obtained similar results. After about 10 minutes, students can come to the conclusion that a lower number of camouflaged dots were picked up. The reason why it takes a while is that students had different colored environments; likewise, different colored dots were camouflaged. While students are discussing, walk around the room listening to conversations. This is an opportunity to see if there were discrepancies among students' results. For example, one time a student did not follow directions and purposefully tried to pick up the same colored dots as the paper.

After students compare results, bring the discussion to the whole class level. Ask critical questions such as "What did you find?" "Were your findings similar or dissimilar to your neighbors?" "What do the findings mean?" and "Which colored mice are most likely to survive, the ones that are the same or different colored from the environment?" Students understand that the mice that are the same color as the environment are more likely to survive; however, the idea is that the mice remaining in the environment are the ones that will be reproducing. This is, in fact, natural selection.

Next, discuss students' results and findings utilizing a whole group discussion activity. Start the discussion by asking, "Why don't we see blue mice, yellow mice, pink mice, and green mice in nature?" During the whole group discussion, students can explain that mice with very contrasting colors to the environment will die from predation. Taking this conversation one step further, "Would there be an array of mice colors in the next generation?" Students think a bit, and then respond, "Probably not; only the mice who survive predation are the ones that look like their environment. The next generation will look like the mice that survived." The inheritability of traits is exactly what student explorations were intended to point out. Next ask, "Why wouldn't there be hawks in nature that contrast with the environment?" This will take students a little more time to figure out, but one student will light up and explain, "Hawks have to blend into their environment so they will not be seen. If the hawk is seen, then the mice will run away and the hawk will not be able to hunt."

In continuing with the Explain phase, tell your class that organisms are naturally selected for and against. In the case of the mice, mice that were the same color as their environment lived, and in nature, they would be able to reproduce. Mice with colors that highly contrasted with the environment are less likely to reproduce. In effect, organisms that are camouflaged are "selected" for, and organisms that do not exhibit camouflage are "selected" against. When the environment favors one characteristic of an organism, this characteristic will occur in higher frequency in the next generation. Environmental selection is one way a population will evolve. This is a type of natural selection. The change in the characteristics of an organism is not initiated by the organism but is initiated by variations in the physical traits of organisms, and some of the characteristics provide more of an advantage, such as blending into the environment, compared to others. The environment and the variation in survival abilities is the impetus for natural section. Likewise, predators experience the same type of selection. One result of natural selection results in physical characteristics we call camouflage. Finally, show the YouTube video, "Wildlife in Disguise: Amazing Animal Camouflage" (Yee 2009).

Elaboration Phase
The Elaboration is intended to introduce the idea of mimicry and its advantages. To demonstrate mimicry, re-create the prior activity with an additional five light-blue dots (made from hole punching standard light-blue computer paper), for a total of 25 dots. Instead of students trying to pick up any of these dots, they must stay away from the light-blue dots; otherwise, it will kill the hawk. If a student picks up a light-blue dot by accident, the hawk dies, and he or she must quit the game for that trial. Again, have students fill out the data table; however, it is only necessary for students to answer questions one and two on the worksheet (Appendix A). Students see that although that the number of edible mice (20) remained constant from activity one, fewer dots of all colors were picked

up. This phenomenon is most evident with the blue dots. Ask, "Why couldn't you pick up as many mice compared to the first activity?" A student responds, "Because either the hawk died because I picked up a light blue one, or I was spending too much time avoiding the light blue ones I could not quickly pick up the others."

Day 3

Evaluation Phase

In the Evaluation phase, students research examples of natural selection and color variations within a population. Start by projecting a range of pictures of animals exhibiting color variation—for example, the Eastern gray squirrel. The Eastern gray squirrel can exhibit several different colors from gray, brown, and white to black. Ask students, "Have you ever seen a black squirrel before?" Likely most of them have not since black squirrels, though once more prevalent in North America, are now few and far between. Black squirrels once occurred at a much higher frequency compared to today. Using this example, explain to students that in the 1600s and 1700s, the United States consisted of high-density forests perfect for shading the black phase squirrel. Since then, with increased numbers of humans hunting from the forest floor (instead of hawks from overhead), it was relatively easy to see the outlines of the black phase squirrel compared to the other colors. The increased predation by humans decreased the frequency of the black phase squirrels and likewise increased the frequency of the gray to brownish-gray squirrel (Hamilton 2002).

Next, students will get to do some group research. Pass out a handout (Appendix B) that will guide students through the research process. Go through each question before dividing students into groups of no more than three to research an animal that exhibits camouflage. Students work together using a worksheet to guide their investigation. Third graders do surprisingly well locating information on the Internet.

After doing the necessary research to answer the guiding questions, student groups present their research on a poster board. Student groups print pictures from the Internet, use colors, markers, and glue sticks to create a visual to hang up and share with the class. On the poster board, students provide information regarding camouflage and the organism's environment, along with color variation among organisms. When groups present, it is essential they explain why populations of this animal appear camouflaged and if there are color variations of the animal, and why some colors are a better fit for survival. In general, the third graders love this and do quite well with the presentations.

Conclusions

Elementary students enjoy learning about natural selection and mimicry. By following the 5E Constructivist Model, students are engaged in activities, explore and process thoughts and ideas, are eager to discuss their findings, can elaborate on their understanding of the topic, are excited to research animals exhibiting camouflage and mimicry, and can demonstrate their knowledge of camouflage and mimicry via oral presentations. We have found this lesson to be engaging and fun for the children, all the while meeting state and national standards.

Resources

Yee, L. 2009. *Wildlife in disguise: Amazing animal camouflage*. Earth Touch. www. youtube. com/watch?v=uaYbcN7Wa M (accessed November 13, 2012).

References

Bybee, R.W. 1997. *Achieving scientific literacy: From purposes to practices*. Portsmouth, NH: Heinemann Educational Books, Inc.
Collins, J. 2010. Camouflage lessons for middle school students. www.helium.com/items/1810902-animals-scienceexperiment-camouflage-video (accessed May 13, 2012).
Hamilton, W. 2002. The virtual nature trail and Penn State New Kensington. www.psu.edu/dept/nkbiology/naturetrail/species pages/specieslist.htm (accessed December 9, 2013).
Josephs, M. 2011. Color changing dots. *Scientific American*, May 11. www.scientificamerican.com/article.cfm?id = color-changing- dots-bring-science-home (accessed July 4, 2013).
National Research Council (NRC). 1996. *National science education standards*. Washington, DC: The National Academies Press.
National Research Council (NRC). 2000. *Inquiry and the national science education standards: A guide for teaching and learning*. Washington, DC: The National Academies Press.
National Research Council (NRC). 2012. *A framework for K—12 science education: Practices, crosscutting concepts, and core concepts*. Washington, DC: The National Academies Press.
National Research Council (NRC). 2013. *Next generation science standards: For states, by states*. Washington, DC: The National Academies Press.

Appendix A: Sheet Students Use to Record Data

Directions: Record the number of yellow, green, pink, and blue dots picked up and the number left on the paper after 10 seconds.

My environment color is:

Trial 1 Data

Yellow Mice		Green Mice		Pink Mice		Blue Mice	
Picked Up	Left	Picked Up	Left	Picked Up	Left	Picked Up	Left

Trial 2 Data

Yellow Mice		Green Mice		Pink Mice		Blue Mice	
Picked Up	Left	Picked Up	Left	Picked Up	Left	Picked Up	Left

Trial 3 Data

Yellow Mice		Green Mice		Pink Mice		Blue Mice	
Picked Up	Left	Picked Up	Left	Picked Up	Left	Picked Up	Left

Average Number of Yellow Mice Picked Up
Average Number of Green Mice Picked Up
Average Number of Pink Mice Picked Up
Average Number of Blue Mice Picked Up

Follow-Up Questions

1. What color of environment did you have?
2. What was the average number of yellow, green, pink, and blue mice picked up?
3. Which color of mice was hardest to pick up in your environment?

4. How would your results have been different if you had a different colored environment? Why?
5. Compare your results with someone who had a different colored environment than you. Do your classmate's results differ from yours? If so, why? If not, why not?
6. Why do you think in nature there is not a wide variety of colored mice?

Appendix B: Worksheet Students Fill Out in Groups of Three for the Evaluation Phase

What is the name of the animal you picked to research?
Where does the animal live? What does its environment look like?
What does this animal look like?
Can this animal vary in color? (Example: Wolves have a range in color from white, gray, to all black.)
How does the animal behave?
Does it sleep at night and hunt during the day?
What does the animal eat?
How does the animal find food?
Is there an animal that hunts the animal you are researching? If yes, what?
For the animal you are researching, is there some reason why one color would be a better fit for survival than another color? Explain.

11

Lessons Learned

Patrick Brown and James Concannon

Instructional planning is much more a deliberate process than just identifying activities to use with students. The manner in which we sequence activities, how we have students explore their world, and the phenomenon we home in on to focus instruction are essential to ensure students learn the intended material. The process of incorporating the NGSS into practice can be achieved by using the design principles illustrated in the model lessons. The beginning chapters of this book and the model lessons have been an attempt to start the conversation about what effective teaching and learning looks like in real-life settings. We have tried to encourage your professional growth by connecting you with some of the research in science education and model lessons that illustrate the research in practice. Here we share three brief lessons learned from designing and implementing the model lessons with students.

Lesson 1

Explore-before-explain instructional sequences tap into students' innate curiosity and cultivate their abilities to do and know science. We have worked with many teachers who are nervous about letting students explore science at the onset of an instructional unit. These teachers comment that students need "mini" lectures and prior instruction on content for students to be successful. Explaining content first is counterproductive for many reasons. First, many novice science learners have no framework in which to contextualize new knowledge. Second, learning content that is disconnected from firsthand experiences contributes to students viewing content and practices as being separate.

Students need to interact with materials and objects in the real world to have a framework for building science knowledge. Because, as learners, all of us try to fit new experiences with what we already know. Once students have experience, they need chances to make evidence-based claims and have official explanations. After all, learning is more than just "hands-on"; students need "minds-on" opportunities to construct knowledge in supportive environments. It makes sense that we will most readily learn if we can find the proper fit between our firsthand experiences and science knowledge.

Lesson 2

Becoming an inquiry classroom is all about adopting a less-is-more approach to teaching. It is impossible and unnecessary to cover the amount of content found in most textbooks. Thus, inquiry-based approaches require teachers to focus on the most critical topics beneficial for lifelong science understanding. Once teachers have focused learning objectives on desired content, students need chances to explore content on a deep level through direct experiences that use part or all of the essential features of inquiry and the appropriate variation. From engaging in inquiry activities, students develop robust ideas about the natural world and valid and reliable ways to generate knowledge. The rewards of using inquiry cannot be highlighted enough. Inquiry leads to higher achievement, improved attitudes, and greater abilities to think logically and reason about data and evidence and science knowledge. Thus, inquiry-based approaches are an essential foundation for classroom instruction and cultivate the skills necessary to becoming learners who are more self-reliant.

Lesson 3

Teachers can motivate deep student learning by framing experiences around a real-life scenario or phenomenon. Phenomena provide for many learning activities and offer the chance for students to develop deep conceptual understanding. Most importantly, within a phenomenon-based instructional approach, students have immediate chances to explore science rather than receiving knowledge directly from the teacher. If students view scientific knowledge as being utterly unrelated to their lives, they are not likely to remember it or view it as necessary. Homing in on phenomena that are relevant to drive instruction helps students understand the intended content and make connections between supporting ideas. Phenomenon-based teaching helps students construct an extensive network of understanding. The result is that students can better transfer knowledge and skills between topics in the area of study and among other science disciplines. Students who engage in phenomenon-based activities have an understanding of how science relates to their everyday lives and the larger overarching concepts, as well as making connections to smaller, supporting ideas.

Conclusions

Changing our practice to address the NGSS may require us to look inward and consider why some approaches are more beneficial than others. The more we can help students make connections between their firsthand experiences with data and the claims they construct, the better they will know science and be able to use science in their lives. As you contemplate the model lessons and information presented in the introductory chapters, keep in mind that the 21st century demands innovative ways of problem solving and critical thinking within a content area. When you have time in your classroom, take a moment to think about your next lessons. Questions should come to mind such as, "Do my students have firsthand experiences with science before teacher explanations?" "Do I use inquiry in my daily practices?" and "What phenomena drive my lessons?" This exercise will help you bridge the skills necessary to be successful in today's society with the research on how students learn science best. Right now, you are working toward developing a more professional practice that will benefit for students for the long term. We wish you the best of luck as you continue growing your repertoire of instructional practices that take students to higher levels of learning.

For Product Safety Concerns and Information please contact our EU
representative GPSR@taylorandfrancis.com
Taylor & Francis Verlag GmbH, Kaufingerstraße 24, 80331 München, Germany

www.ingramcontent.com/pod-product-compliance
Lightning Source LLC
Chambersburg PA
CBHW082052230426
43670CB00016B/2869